Titles in Judson Press's "Living Church" Series

Available now...
Making Friends, Making Disciples:
Growing Your Church through Authentic Relationships
Lee B. Spitzer

Caring Pastors, Caring People:
Equipping Your Church for Pastoral Care
Marvin A. McMickle

Coming in Fall 2012...
Lay Learners, Lay Leaders:
Tapping the Root for Ministry
Susan Gillies and M. Ingrid Dvirnak

D1316248

www.judsonpress.com / 800-4-JUDSON

Caring Pastors, Caring People

Equipping Your Church for Pastoral Care

MARVIN A. McMICKLE
J. DWIGHT STINNETT, SERIES EDITOR

JUDSON PRESS
PUBLISHERS SINCE 1824
VALLEY FORGE, PA

Caring Pastors, Caring People
Equipping Your Church for Pastoral Care
© 2011 by Judson Press, Valley Forge, PA 19482-0851
All rights reserved.

Unless otherwise noted, the Scripture quotations contained herein are from the New Revised Standard Version of the Bible, copyright 1989, by the Division of Christian Education of the National Council of Churches in the U.S.A. Used by permission. All rights reserved.

Scripture quotations marked NIV are taken from the Holy Bible, *New International Version®, NIV®.* Copyright © 1973, 1978, 1984, 2011 by Biblica, Inc.™ Used by permission of Zondervan. All rights reserved worldwide.

Interior design by Wendy Ronga, Hampton Design Group. Cover design by Tobias Becker and Birdbox Graphic Design (www.birdboxdesign.com)

Library of Congress Cataloging-in-Publication Data
McMickle, Marvin Andrew.
Caring pastors, caring people: equipping your church for pastoral care / Marvin A. McMickle. — 1st ed.
p. cm. — (Living church series)
ISBN 978-0-8170-1700-2 (pbk.: alk. paper) 1. Pastoral care. 2. Church work. 3. Caring—Religious aspects—Christianity. 4. Helping behavior—Religious aspects—Christianity. 5. Pastoral theology. I. Title.
BV4011.3.M43 2011
259.086—dc23   2011022644

Printed in the U.S.A.
First Edition, 2011.

Contents

Series Preface

Living
Church

"What happened? Just a few years ago we were a strong church. We had thriving ministries and supported a worldwide mission effort. Our community knew us, and cared about what we did. Now we are not sure if we can survive another year." It is a painful conversation I have had with more church leaders than I can name here.

I explained how images like *meltdown, tsunami, earthquake,* and *storm* have been used to describe the crisis that has been developing for the North American church over the last 25 years. Our present crisis is underscored by the American Religious Identification Survey 2008. Not just this church, but nearly every church is being swamped by the changes.

Volumes have already been written in analysis of the current situation and in critique of the church. I suggested a few books and workshops that I knew, trying to avoid the highly technical work. But the church leader I was talking with was overwhelmed by all the analysis. "Yes, I am sure that is true. But what do we do? When I look at what is happening and I hear all the criticism, I wonder if the church has a future at all. Do we deserve one?"

I emphasized that there are no simple answers, and that those who offer simplistic solutions are either deceived or deceiving. There is no "church cookbook" for today. (I'm not sure there ever really was one.) I tried to avoid an equally simplistic pietistic answer.

Still, the church leader pressed. "So, is the church dead? Do we just need to schedule a funeral and get over it? We are all so tired and frustrated."

I said that I did not accept the sentiment of futility and despair about the future of the church. I believe the church is alive and persists not because of what we do, but because of what God has done and continues to do in the church.

The pain was real, as were the struggle and the longing. I wanted to help this church leader understand, but not be overwhelmed by, the peculiar set of forces impacting the church today. But information was not enough. I wanted to encourage church leaders with specific things that could be done, without implying that success was guaranteed or that human effort was sufficient. I wanted them to learn from what others are doing, not to mechanically copy them, but to use what others are doing as lenses to look closely at their own context. I wanted them to avoid all the churchy labels that are out there, and be a living church in their community, empowered and sustained by the living God.

Those of us who work with larger groupings of churches and pay attention to the things that are happening around us know that several forces are having a devastating affect on the church today. There are eight key areas where the impact has been especially acute.

These include biblical illiteracy, financial pressures, overwhelming diversity, shrinking numbers, declining leadership base, brokenness in and around us, an increasing inward focus, and the unraveling of spiritual community. It is not hard to see how each of these is interrelated with the others.

Living Church is a new series from Judson Press intended to address each of these forces from a congregational perspective. While our authors are well-informed biblically, theologically, and topically, this is not intended to be an exercise in ecclesiastical academics. Our intent is to empower congregational leaders (both clergy and lay) to rise to the challenge before us.

Our goal is not merely to lament our state of crisis, but to identify key contributors for our time and place so that we can move on to effective responses. Our time and place is the American Church in the twenty-first century.

The first volume in this series, *Making Friends, Making Disciples*, by Dr. Lee Spitzer, addressed the issue of shrinking numbers by reminding us of the spiritual discipline of being and making friends, not with some ulterior motive, but because God has called us to relationship.

This second volume, *Caring Pastors, Caring People*, by Dr. Marvin McMickle, confronts the growing brokenness within and around the church from a pastoral perspective. I can think of no one better to address this issue. Here is a person with an authentic pastor's heart. That is evident when Marvin launches this book with a reflection on Thomas Oden's suggestion that the key task of any pastor is "learning properly to shepherd the flock of God."

Dr. McMickle describes an expansive practice of pastoral care that goes way beyond "pastoral counseling" and becomes the "overarching premise that encompasses, permeates, informs, and inspires all ministry tasks performed by the pastor." But this task is not the sole property of the pastor. One of the tasks of the pastor is to equip others in the congregation to the task of pastoral care.

While "a caring pastor is at the heart of the process," Rev. McMickle envisions pastoral care as three concentric circles. The innermost circle includes those tasks and skills that are appropriately linked to the office of pastor. The second circle of pastoral care is the congregation caring for one another. The outer circle is "the congregation extending itself to the people and problems outside the walls of the local church."

For me, this is one of the most distinctive features of Marvin's theology of ministry. Work outside the congregation is not merely about humanitarianism, social work, evangelism, or even justice. It is first and foremost a matter of pastoral care. And it is not optional.

A deep love for the church is evident as Dr. McMickle opens his pastor's heart to us through personal experiences, biblical reflection, theological analysis, and practical examples. I believe his answer to the overwhelming brokenness we see in and around the church is found in his three circles of care. First, pastors must assume the appropriate role of pastor, practicing and equipping others for pastoral care. Second, the congregation must exercise mutual pastoral care within the faith community. Finally, the congregation must assume pastoral care responsibility for its neighbors. Truly, "a caring church is a living church."

—Rev. Dr. J. Dwight Stinnett
Series Editor
Executive Minister
American Baptist Churches,
Great Rivers Region

Three Circles of Care—
A Model for Ministry

CHAPTER 1

Learning to Shepherd the Flock of God

He tends his flock like a shepherd:
He gathers the lambs in his arms
and carries them close to his heart;
he gently leads those that have young.
—Isaiah 40:11 (NIV)

In his book *Pastoral Theology*, Thomas C. Oden suggests that one of the chief tasks of any pastor of a local church is "learning properly to shepherd the flock of God."[1] That statement deserves considerable reflection by those who feel called to pastoral ministry, as well as by the congregations with whom they work. What exactly is entailed in "learning properly to shepherd the flock of God"? Oden sets this observation within the context of reminding the reader that we commonly expect other groups of professionals to possess a core set of skills that inform them as they go about their duties. He says, "One would expect physicians or attorneys to have grasped an integral theory of their task, some overarching conception of their official duty, before beginning their practice."[2] He then says that many people enter into ministry "without any such great conception or overarching vision."[3] Not only that, but many churches make decisions about what they expect from their pastor without seeking from their pool of candidates or the person presently serving in that position anything that approaches "a conception or overarching vision" that would inform them in the exercise of their duties. In light of the characteristics and qualifications expected of other groups of professionals, Oden says, "The importance of the office of pastor still quietly pleads with us to think with extraordinary care about the better and worse ways in which that office might be conceived and practiced."[4]

Three Circles of Pastoral Care as a Model for Ministry

In this book, pastoral care is conceived as that general conception or overarching vision for how all ministry tasks can and should be conducted within the context of local churches. We are at a time when church growth is declining in all but a few Christian communities. We are also at a point where the influence of pastors both inside and outside the church is steadily diminishing due to the increasingly secular and "spiritual" nature of our postmodern world. This book, written with these realities in mind, offers an approach to pastoral care and the ministry of the local church that can assist pastors in learning properly how to shepherd the body of Christ.

Pastoral care should be understood as the umbrella term under which a wide variety of ministry tasks are grouped, all of them done for the nurture and support of the congregation. Pastoral care is not simply one of the many tasks performed by persons who serve in pastoral ministry. Instead, pastoral care is the paradigm in which all ministry acts are performed. Pastoral care should not be viewed solely as what happens when the pastor sits with individuals or families in crisis times. Nor should it be limited to what happens when persons come to the pastor's study for counsel. Instead, pastoral care is discussed here as care and concern that are manifested in every aspect of a pastor's work. Pastoral care is the overarching premise that encompasses, permeates, informs, and inspires all ministry tasks performed by the pastor. Whether preparing and delivering sermons, making hospital calls, presiding at weddings and funerals, or planning programs for the upcoming church year, a caring pastor is at the heart of the process.

Isaiah 40:11 says the Lord, who is our pastoral example, "tends his flock like a shepherd." That phrase does not point primarily to any one task performed by the shepherd on behalf of the sheep. Instead, it points to the spirit and attitude by which all aspects of the work of a shepherd should be approached. Shepherds feed the sheep, guide them through the desert, and protect them from dangers that range from the thickets in which they might get caught to the wolves that may attack the flock. Sometimes the shepherd uses a staff to prod the sheep along in the right direction. Sometimes that same staff is used to rescue a sheep that may have fallen into a place from which it cannot get out by its own strength. To tend the flock like a shepherd is not to do just one single task for the sheep, but to implement an overarching vision of care for the sheep. This is the first way in which pastoral care is discussed under this model.

A second aspect of this model of pastoral care makes an even greater break with the traditional understanding of the term: pastoral care is not limited to the work of the clergy. The same spirit of caring and compassion with which pastors go about their work is expected of the congregation. Pastoral care may begin with a caring pastor who interacts with individuals and families in the church, but it must be extended to include the work of the laity. Members of the local church must be equipped and encouraged to care for one another instead of waiting for the pastor to show up and do all the work.

A third aspect of pastoral care is equally important in this paradigm: a caring congregation extending itself to the people and problems outside the walls of the local church. Some people might be inclined to think of this area of a church's ministry as social outreach or benevolence. And others might think that local congregations need not be involved with the world beyond the walls of the church at all.

I set forth the exact opposite argument: God will judge the church as much for what it does to impact and influence life outside its walls as for what it does when tucked safely inside the sanctuary. A caring congregation refuses to be limited solely to its own issues and concerns. When pastors have learned properly to shepherd the flock of God, as Oden suggests they should, churches will sense the necessity of reaching out beyond their membership to impact the people and problems outside their walls with care and concern and Christian love.

This model for pastoral care is based on the visual image of three concentric circles moving in a steadily outward direction, just as concentric ripples form when a rock is thrown in a pond. These concentric circles suggest that there are some aspects of pastoral care that rightfully and necessarily belong to the pastor of a congregation. Certain tasks and the skills required to perform them belong to pastors by virtue of the office they occupy. That arena of activity constitutes the first circle of pastoral circle.

That being said, a person who has learned properly to shepherd the flock of God has developed an overarching vision of the ministry that allows for and expects that at many points members of the congregation need to be equipped and encouraged to provide care for one another. Every church should establish the expectation that the pastor should not do all the work of the church alone. Therefore, the second concentric circle of pastoral care is when the church is willing and able to care for one another out of a deep sense of mutual concern fueled by Christian love.

A third circle of pastoral care needs to be established if pastors are properly to shepherd the flock of God. An overarching vision of ministry is one that pushes the ministry concerns of the church outward beyond its own walls and membership. As concentric

Pastoral Care: 3 Concentric Circles of Care

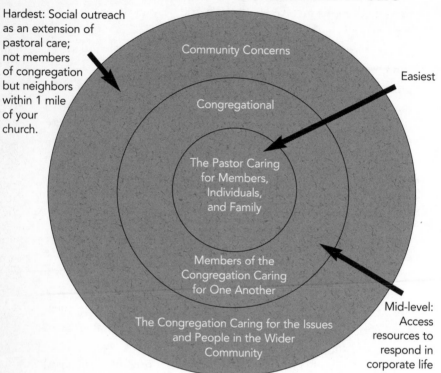

Hardest: Social outreach as an extension of pastoral care; not members of congregation but neighbors within 1 mile of your church.

Community Concerns

Congregational

The Pastor Caring for Members, Individuals, and Family

Members of the Congregation Caring for One Another

The Congregation Caring for the Issues and People in the Wider Community

Easiest

Mid-level: Access resources to respond in corporate life

circles move steadily outward, so must the ministry of local churches move steadily outward from the pastor caring for the congregation to members of the congregation caring for one another and finally to the congregation as a whole caring for the people and problems that exist outside its doors and beyond its own members.

Thus, any pastor wanting to know how to shepherd the flock of God properly should operate with this overarching idea in mind. Employ the image of three concentric circles where the work of the ministry is always flowing outward—from the pastor outward to the congregation and from the congregation outward to the wider community. All three circles are required if the work of the church is to be accomplished. Stated another way, something of importance is missing in the life of any church when the pastor is the only person showing care and concern for others or when the care and concern the congregation does show is limited to those who are active church members. A healthy church is one in which all three of these circles of care are operating at the same time and with equal emphasis.

Theory Should Come before Practice

The larger portion of this book focuses on the practical tasks of ministry that should normally occupy pastors and congregations. However, as Ray S. Anderson points out in *The Shape of Practical Theology*, those who engage in the practice of ministry must be sure that their practice is informed by some theory that undergirds and informs the work they are doing. There must be a biblical and theological "why" that explains and justifies the "what" in which they are engaged. Anderson sees practical theology as filling that role. He says, "The primary purpose of practical theology is to ensure that the church's public proclamations and praxis in the world faithfully reflect the nature and purpose of God's continuing mission to the world and in so doing authentically addresses the contemporary context into which the church seeks to minister."[5] Within the concentric circles model, the circles of pastoral care constitute the praxis for ministry; they set forth what must be done and by whom. What must be added is the underlying theory that gives a reason for why we should do certain things in ministry. Without a clear theory that informs a consistent practice, our ministry can quickly become unfocused and inconsistent.

What Constitutes Effectiveness in Ministry?

When you think about pastoral theology as the overarching vision or pastoral care as the skills needed to shepherd the flock of God, you might be inclined to think about one person offering services and support to many people, as when a single shepherd cares for and leads an entire flock of sheep. This would be especially true were you to maintain the comparison of pastors to physicians or attorneys who as professionals assume the lead role while the patient or client is largely the "beneficiary of services rendered." Any pastor who operates with that philosophy of ministry is not properly shepherding his or her flock!

Throughout this volume, one point above all others is underscored: when pastoral leadership is based on one "expert" leader doing all the work, the end result will be a complacent, consumer-oriented congregation that expects only the pastor to engage in the work of the ministry. Thus, I offer one concise answer to the question of how pastors should properly shepherd the flock of God: *do not to attempt to do the work alone.* Rather than assuming sole responsibility for this task (whether due to the leader's ego or the congregation's expectations), pastors would do well to employ a different model. The circles of pastoral care model is designed to equip and encourage each member within the flock of God to assume some personal responsibility for the care of those both inside and beyond the walls of the local church. We now turn to the biblical passages that provide the theory on which the circles of care rest.

Equipping the Church for the Work of the Ministry

The first and most important step in learning properly to shepherd the flock of God is to base that approach to ministry on a firm biblical foundation. In Ephesians 4:11-13, Paul sets forth a model for effectively and efficiently shepherding the flock of God from which every Christian congregation in this country and around the world could benefit. The essence of Paul's message is the essence of the three concentric circles; rather than doing all of the work themselves, pastors should continuously equip the church to be involved in ministry. Paul says in this passage that some are gifted to be apostles, some prophets, some evangelists, and some pastors and teachers. It is this fourth group, pastors and teachers, with which this book is chiefly concerned. The concentric circles of care model described in the pages that follow is meant to help pastors and teachers in "learning properly to shepherd the flock of God."

What Is the Role of Pastors and Teachers? — In the early church, the persons Paul references in the first three categories (apostles, prophets, and evangelists) are persons whose gifts were intended to be exercised within the context of the universal church. They exercised their spiritual gifts wherever they went. No one better embodied this reality than the apostle Paul himself. However, as Francis Foulkes suggests, the phrase "pastors and teachers" "describes the ministers of the local church."[6] Foulkes points out that these two tasks are linked together. "Pastors and teachers were gifted to be responsible for the day-to-day building up of the church."[7] The linking of these two tasks in a single person is reinforced by 1 Timothy 3:2 where Paul says that every pastor must be "an apt teacher."

Learning properly to shepherd the flock of God means that clergy need to exercise their role as pastor and teacher in a way that allows the words of Ephesians 4:12 to be fulfilled. That is, their work should result in the equipping of the saints for the work of the ministry and for building up the body of Christ. Pheme Perkins picks up on this point: "Although the particular offices refer to those who are in charge of guiding churches after the apostle's death, Ephesians assumes that all Christians are part of the building process. Maturity involves the community as a whole, not merely particular individuals."[8]

Walter Liefeld adds another dimension to this discussion of pastors who equip members to do the work of the ministry. He talks about the persons listed in verse 11 as those who have been gifted to perform a certain function in the life of the church. "The gifted leaders equip the people, who in turn do the works of service, which in turn results in the building up of the body of Christ."[9] When viewed through the lens of this passage, Liefeld states unequivocally that rather than doing all the work themselves, "It is clear that the leaders have the responsibility of preparing others."[10]

James Montgomery Boice served as a pastor at Tenth Presbyterian Church in Philadelphia for more than twenty years. He says that he found Ephesians 4:11-13 to be the organizational principle that accounted for the long-term success of that ministry. He demonstrates how the people referenced in verse 11 can and should interact with those referenced in verse 12. "Instead of giving three tasks to the minister it gives one task to the clergy (equip the saints) and another to the laity (do the work of the ministry). As a result of both fulfilling their proper, God-given function, the body of Christ may be built up."[11] When this approach to ministry is embraced, it can result in what Boice later refers to as "every member ministry."[12] That is precisely what the three concentric circles of pastoral care seek to create within local churches—a context in which every member shares in the ministry.

Pastors Must Be Intentional about This Model— Pastors must cover many topics over the course of a year's work in ministry. Stewardship plans have to be developed and implemented. Discipleship and spiritual formation efforts must be undertaken. Various denominational and doctrinal distinctives need to be taught or supported. While all of these areas of ministry and many more must be attended to, it is crucial that pastors not neglect the words of Ephesians 4:12 by failing to equip the saints for the work of the ministry. To that end, time must be invested in planning sermons, Bible studies, special programs, and motivational events that have this outcome as their primary objective.

In other words, the main task of pastors who have learned properly to shepherd the flock of God is not simply to immerse themselves in a multitude of priestly and pastoral tasks while the congregation remains unchallenged and unengaged. Instead, pastors must prioritize their work in such a way that as a result of their efforts, church members are being equipped, empowered, and encouraged to do the work of the ministry and to build up the body of Christ. One of the ways by which this approach to ministry can be done is through the use of the three concentric circles of pastoral care. Under this model, responsibility for the work of the ministry is steadily being pushed in an outward direction, from the pastor caring for the congregation, to congregation members caring for one another, and finally to the congregation showing care and concern for the people and problems in the surrounding community.

A Visual Image or Acronym Can Be Useful— To help our congregation at Antioch Baptist Church of Cleveland where I served for twenty-four years create a model of ministry that embraced the principles set forth so far in this book, we used the acronym TOWER. That church happens to have a tall brick, Gothic-style tower as part of its architectural design, which can be seen from a great distance and is the feature by which the church is most readily identified. We decided to use that familiar architectural feature as the concept around which to structure our philosophy of ministry. That philosophy not only served to help the pastor properly shepherd the flock of God, but it also allowed the congregation to design an approach to ministry in which the three concentric circles of care could be employed.

Here is how the acronym TOWER works:

T is our teaching ministry that covers all forms of traditional Christian education.

O is our outreach into the community through a variety of hands-on ministry efforts.

W is our worship and involves those times when the church is open for that purpose.

E is our evangelism and focuses on spreading the gospel through radio, TV, and revivals.

R is our relationships and is the rubric under which we support and care for each other.

This acronym appears on banners that hang throughout the church building. It is featured on the back of the church bulletin on a weekly basis, and a picture of the TOWER appears on the church letterhead as well as on all staff business cards. The church staff is organized so that a member of the clergy team is assigned to each one of the areas of ministry in TOWER. The church budget is designed so that each area of the TOWER has its own line items. Finally, lay members of the congregation are elected at the annual church meeting to provide leadership in and/or support each of these five ministry areas. Of course, persons can volunteer to be involved in any ministry areas of the church that are of interest to them. However, a core of elected lay leaders provides a reliable basis on which to operate our TOWER.

The TOWER Gives Shape to Three Circles of Care— Through the use of the TOWER acronym as an organizational principle for ministry, the congregation has been able to actualize the three circles of pastoral care with good effect. Through teaching, relationships, and worship, the pastor is able to shepherd the flock of God. Each area of the TOWER concept, but especially relationships, has afforded opportunities for members of the congregation to actively reach out and care for one another in times of need. Through the ministry of outreach, the church has been able to extend itself into the surrounding community through an HIV/AIDS testing and support program, a hunger center and food pantry, three Alcoholics Anonymous groups, a credit union for persons who have not been well received by traditional banks, and a tithing program through which our congregation tithes out to various community-based and national organizations 10 percent of our annual church budget.

Every congregation should give some thought to the creation of some acronym, slogan, mission statement, or organizing principle around which their work as a congregation can be constructed. Obviously, that organizing principle should involve a caring pastor who is determined to shepherd the flock of God in such a way that church members care for one another and that they also be equipped and encouraged to care for the people and the problems that exist outside the walls of their church building.

Caring for One Another Is an Ancient Biblical Model

While the use of the image of circles of care is unique to this book, the idea of urging the church to share in the work of the ministry is as old as the words of Peter to the early Christian community in Jerusalem in Acts 6:1-6. A dispute erupted within that church over the unfair and/or prejudicial distribution of commonly held goods. The Hellenistic Jews came to the apostles with the complaint that their widows were not being treated on a par with the widows of the Hebraic Jews. The resolution was the earliest example in the life of the Christian church of people being equipped to do the work of the ministry.

Rather than being sucked into yet another responsibility, Peter suggested that the church identify seven persons who were filled with the Holy Spirit, who possessed wisdom, and who enjoyed a good reputation within the community. Once those persons had been identified, they were to be brought before the apostles who would consecrate them and publicly give them responsibility for caring for the widows. While those seven persons engaged in the work of the ministry, the apostles would continue to devote themselves to the ministry of the Word and to prayer. Those persons must have performed their task effectively, because nothing more is mentioned for the remainder of the book of Acts about those widows being neglected.

Here is a clear instance in which the apostles equipped the saints for the work of the ministry. It was done in a way that allowed their preaching and teaching ministry to continue, while the administrative and benevolence work of the community that had to be performed was accomplished by others in the body of Christ. Peter was careful not to resolve the dispute while those who raised the concern simply stood by and watched. He demonstrated in word and deed that the work of the ministry was to be shared by the whole body of Christ. This is a lesson every pastor needs to learn and every congregation needs to embrace. Pastors and teachers should equip the church to do the work of the ministry. Those listed in Ephesians 4:11 called on those listed in Ephesians 4:12 to embrace the work outlined in Ephesians 4:13. This is a paradigm that people who are called on to be pastors and teachers in the twenty-first century would do well to replicate in their own ministries.

Notes

1. Thomas C. Oden, *Pastoral Theology* (New York: Harper&Row, 1983), 13.
2. Oden, 13.
3. Oden, 13
4. Oden, 13.
5. Ray S. Anderson, *The Shape of Practical Theology: Empowering Ministry with Theological Praxis* (Downers Grove, IL: InterVarsity, 2001), 22.
6. Francis Foulkes, *Ephesians*, Tyndale New Testament Commentaries (Grand Rapids: Eerdmans, 1997), 127.
7. Foulkes, 127.
8. Pheme Perkins, *Ephesians* (Nashville: Abingdon, 1997), 100.
9. Walter Liefeld, *Ephesians* (Downers Grove, IL: InterVarsity, 1997), 106.
10. Liefeld, 106.
11. James Montgomery Boice, *Ephesians* (Grand Rapids: Baker, 1997), 140.
12. Boice, 141.

CHAPTER 2

To Serve This Present Age

"The thief comes only to steal and kill and destroy;
I have come that they may have life,
and have it to the full."
—John 10:10 (NIV)

A Christian hymn includes this line: "To serve this present age my calling to fulfill; O may it all my pow'rs engage to do my Master's will!"[1] Pastors would do well to consider the implications of this hymn when learning properly to shepherd the flock of God using the Ephesians 4:11-13 model. Some major obstacles exist "in this present age" that must be overcome by pastors who seek to equip the church to do the work of the ministry. In far too many churches, nothing remotely close to the Ephesians 4:11-13 model is happening.

The church in America seems to be passing through an era when people are fixated on a gospel of personal benefit, a consumer Christianity where the issue is "What's in it for me?" That understanding of the gospel swings out on the hinges of individual salvation and then swings back on the hinges of prosperity theology. Such an understanding of the nature and purpose of the church is a great impediment when it comes to persuading people in the church that they have a role to play beyond "being blessed."

In both the quest for personal salvation and the pursuit of material prosperity, the objective in church life is to discover what the church can provide. Little if any attention is given to the question of what the people should be doing in service to the church and in service to the kingdom of God. In churches where these two themes are given preeminent attention, one seldom if ever hears a word about pastors equipping the church to do the work of the ministry. If pastors are truly to serve this present age, they must come face-to-face with this problem and approach their ministry in such a way as to counteract these corrupting influences within the body of Christ. Otherwise, it will be nearly impossible to convince "consumer Christians" that they should be sharing in the workload of the church to some significant degree.

The Problem of the Flock of God Being Fleeced and Not Fed
Part of what has shaped this present age is the influence of hour upon hour of Christian radio and TV broadcasts that leave listeners with the clear impression that all God is interested in doing is saving people from their sins and then blessing those same people with material wealth. According to this prosperity gospel, believers receive not only a kind of heaven on earth, but the assurance that even more blessings await them when they die and go to heaven. So much attention is being given to prosperity theology in the twenty-first-century church in America that the distinction between the abundant life of Jesus Christ as set forth in John 10:10 and the "good life" as described by John Locke in eighteenth-century philosophy is hard to find.[2]

People commonly describe their spiritual state as "blessed, healthy, and prosperous." The focus too often seems to be on what God has done for them or on what they believe God has promised to do for them. Of course, all of these blessings come with the caveat that you must sow a seed into a ministry and then have the faith that what you have given will be multiplied and returned to you many times over. Of course, the outcome of this approach to religion is predictable: preachers who are proponents of prosperity theology get rich while the people who "sow seeds" into their ministries get nothing much in return. In these instances, the preacher is not properly shepherding the flock; he or she is simply fleecing the flock!

The Problem of Being Served and Not Serving

It is odd that the proponents of prosperity theology never seem to describe their spiritual state or their spiritual aspiration by saying, "Here am I, send me" (Isaiah 6:8), or as a hymn writer has said, "I am on the battlefield for my Lord." What pastors must make clear as they are learning properly to shepherd the flock of God is that it is not enough for a Christian to say, "I am saved" or "I am blessed." That is an altogether inadequate response when it comes to describing our relationship with God. At some point those declarations of personal salvation and material prosperity become irrelevant, and perhaps even irreverent, if they are not closely followed by the carrying out of the responsibilities that come with discipleship. Pastors must see Ephesians 4:11-13 as their mandate and use their gifts and their office to prepare people to participate in the work of the ministry. And they need to remind their flocks of the clarifying words of Jesus in Matthew 20:28: "The Son of Man did not come to be served but to serve, and to give his life a ransom for many."

The Problem of Consumerism that Corrupts the Church

The local church is not the spiritual equivalent of a drive-thru window where members pull up and place their orders. People should not expect to receive a sermon or a special prayer here and a baptism or baby christening there, and a "super-sized blessing from God" for good measure. Decades ago Harry Emerson Fosdick objected to the idea of turning God into "a cosmic bellhop for whom we can press a button to get things."[3] Unfortunately, this cosmic bellhop approach to church life has been reinforced by the "money-money-money preachers" who push the prosperity gospel. The problem is not simply that this prosperity teaching is a gross distortion of the gospel message as set forth by Jesus, but that it is totally unsupportable by any appeal to Scripture. This has been true from the days of Rev. Frederick Eikerenkoetter (Rev. Ike) in the 1970s to the so-called Word/Faith movement of Kenneth Copeland in the 1980s to the blatant appeal for money and prosperity by Creflo Dollar, Leroy Thompson, and so many others from the 1990s to the present.[4]

There has always been the attempt to make 3 John 1:2 serve the purpose of supporting or even calling for a prosperity theology, but that only works if you accept only the King James Version of that text, which reads, "Beloved, I wish above all things that thou mayest prosper and be in health, even as thy soul prospereth." Those who seek to use this verse to justify consumer Christianity that is disengaged from doing the work of the ministry jump on the word "prosper" as a reinforcement for their theological claim. What they overlook is that the greeting found in that passage was a standard way by which one person wished for the well-being of another person both physically and spiritually.[5] Rather than suggesting God's desire for material wealth and financial prosperity, the real message of this passage is John's hope that "the spiritual progress of Gaius (the recipient of this greeting) will be matched by his physical health and well-being."[6] In other words, 3 John 1:2 is a call for Christian maturity in spiritual formation, not a twenty-first-century version of prosperity theology.

What seems to have happened with what can only be referred to as consumer Christianity is the loss of any focus on spiritual progress or the equipping that needs to be done so that church members stop waiting on material blessings from God and start focusing themselves instead on doing the work of the ministry. However, if that transformation is to happen in this present age, pastors will need to be intentional about equipping the church for ministry. In this spiritual climate, an overarching vision of ministry is needed that counteracts the poisonous effects of a theology that suggests that all God wants from people in the church is that they be spiritually and financially blessed.

A very different message is set forth by Jesus in Matthew 6:33 when he says, "Strive first for the kingdom of God and his righteousness, and all these things will be given to you as well." Jesus calls the church to action and engagement in pursuit of justice and righteousness, not to "sowing a seed" in hopes of receiving a financial blessing in return. This is a common problem pastors have to deal with as they learn properly to shepherd the flock of God.

The Problem of Praise and Worship Alone

Another obstacle for pastors as they seek to serve this present age is the notion that praise and worship done in church on Sunday morning constitutes the full measure of what God requires from us. Every church has people who are more than willing to worship the Lord, gladly standing for extended periods of time lifting up holy hands. They will happily dance and shout under the influence of the Holy Spirit. In some settings they may even be moved to speak in tongues. There is no doubt that God is worthy of our highest praise and worship. Thus, the God we praise and worship is also deserving of the best of our care and compassion for one another, from the members of our own congregation to the people Jesus called "the least of these who are the members of my family" (Matthew 25:40).

I am reminded of the rhythms of the civil rights movement, which revolved around a combination of worship and work. People would gather for worship in the evening, but that time of worship was never an end unto itself. Instead, worship was the means by which people sought to be soothed from the marches and demonstrations for justice in which they had engaged earlier that day as well as the means by which they were strengthened for the renewal of their activities on the following day. The praying, preaching, and singing were exhilarating and uplifting but were never disconnected from the work that had to be done. This point was most recently brought to mind by Bruce Watson's book *Freedom Summer*, which describes how volunteers who came for the voter registration project in Mississippi in 1964 connected work and worship.[7]

A period of praise and worship could easily occupy the average Christian for two to three hours on a Sunday. For many others, especially our Pentecostal, Apostolic, Holiness, and charismatic brothers and sisters, the time for praise and worship could be much longer and much more intense. But neither the length of time nor the intensity involved in praise and worship is an acceptable excuse for not moving from the sanctuary into some form of Christian service as we seek to do the work of the ministry.

Amos 5:18-24 and Micah 6:6-8 make clear that worship alone is not what God desires from people of faith. There is work to be done, and pastors must take up the challenge to equip the church to do the work of the ministry. Too many Christians today are more willing to lift up holy hands to God than they are to extend a helping hand to their brother or sister in the church or in the community.

The Problem of Clergy Burnout

Clergy burnout is a reality in congregations of every denomination across the country. Two things contribute to the high rate of burnout, and I have already discussed one of them—the false belief that clergy should be doing most if not all of the work that goes on in the church.

A troubling trend was announced during the summer of 2010 concerning the high rate of hypertension, depression, and other forms of sickness among clergy in the United States.[8] A study concluded, "These people tend to be driven by a sense of duty to God to answer every call for help from anybody, and they are virtually called upon all the time, 24/7."[9] A pastor from Chicago wrote a letter to the editor of the *New York Times* in response to the story about clergy burnout. That letter said, in part:

> In mainline denominations, where full time is usually defined as 50 or more hours a week, it is generally standard practice to give a church pastor only one day off out of seven. That one day can be lost to a funeral or emergency. In many congregations a pastor who does not postpone or shorten a vacation to tend to a parishioner's emergency or preside at a funeral is derided as uncaring and un-Christian....It is hard to relax when the next phone call may have one dashing home to work.[10]

A second article appeared later that summer that continued to focus on the issue of clergy burnout. This article had less to do with clergy being overworked and more to do with their being told by their congregations exactly how they were expected to perform their tasks.

> The pastoral vocation is to help people grow spiritually, resist their lowest impulses and adopt higher, more compassionate ways. But churchgoers increasingly want pastors to soothe and entertain them....As a result pastors are constantly forced to choose between paths of personal integrity and those that portend greater job security. As religion becomes a consumer experience, the clergy become more unhappy and unhealthy.[11]

A second factor that contributes to clergy burnout is the frustration and anger that develop in many clergy when they try to no avail to involve church members in ministry. Some pastors end up doing too much not because they want to do all the work themselves but because they cannot convince church members to get involved in anything beyond the worship service. If clergy do not assume responsibility for various aspects of church life, the work will simply go undone because no one else feels a responsibility to share in the work.

Embracing the idea of circles of care is a solution to this problem. It reminds everyone involved that while pastoral care may begin with whoever occupies the actual pastoral office in the congregation, the work is not limited to that one pastor. The pastor must, for his or her own health and for the health of the local church, convince church members that they can and should share in the work of pastoral care by first caring for one another. I will give this second circle of care much fuller treatment in chapters 7–9.

Many wonderful resources are available that focus on clergy self-care, and that topic will be given greater attention in chapter 8. I will say here, however, that clergy need to rest and be renewed from the weight of duties in the church and beyond that rightly fall to them.

The Problem of Pastors in Shadows of Scandal and Shame

In 2010–11 three pastors were very much in the news because of their (alleged) actions. Bishop Eddie Long of New Birth Baptist Church in Lithonia, Georgia, was accused of improper sexual conduct with four male members of his congregation. Given his outspoken opposition to homosexuality over the years coupled with his national profile as pastor of a mammoth twenty-five-thousand-member congregation, these accusations against him made national and even international news. I have no idea about the veracity of these charges, and I refused to rush to judgment when the issue was first announced.

My concern was not so much with his guilt or innocence; that will never be fully determined since the matter was resolved out of court with a financial settlement. Rather, I am concerned about what happens to the reputation and credibility of clergy in general when issues like this become media headlines and the topic of conversation in barber shops and beauty salons. Accusations directed at one high-profile pastor often have the effect of causing people already cynical about the church to conclude, "That's the way they all are." The image of the church and the credibility of the clergy both are sullied when nationally known preachers like Eddie Long, Ted Haggard, Jim Bakker, Jimmy Swaggart, and a seemingly endless list of Roman Catholic priests are caught in sexual scandals. These news headlines do not simply impact the accused and his congregation. They are a "black eye" on the church and the clergy who must seek to do ministry within this tainted atmosphere.

An equally troubling pastoral scandal emerged during 2010 and into 2011 involving Rev. Fred Phelps of the Westboro Baptist Church in Kansas. On October 6, 2010, the United States Supreme Court began hearing oral arguments to determine whether Rev. Phelps and members of his congregation have the First Amendment, free speech right to attend the funerals of U.S. soldiers killed in action and make the accusation that their deaths are the result of God's judgment on this country for the sin of homosexuality. To the dismay of many people, the U.S. Supreme Court ruled that the actions of Westboro Baptist Church were considered protected speech under the First Amendment of the U.S. Constitution.

What does it say to the country and to the world when a Christian pastor holds up a sign at a military funeral that says, "Thank God for dead soldiers"? It is difficult to convey the image of the Christian pastor as a person of compassion and agape love when the news is filled with stories about the protests that Phelps is leading across the country. Although he may be legally exercising his right to free speech, he and his colleagues seem to have little regard for how their conduct results in a depiction of Christian pastors as judgmental and intolerant.

A third pastor whose name was in the news for questionable reasons was Terry Jones, leader of a fifty-member congregation in Gainesville, Florida. Jones garnered global media attention and international outrage when he announced plans to burn the Qur'an on September 11, 2010, as a way to commemorate the events of nine years earlier. He garnered even more outrage when he presided over a mock trial that resulted in Islam being "found guilty" of preaching terrorism and the burning of a copy of the Qur'an as an outcome of the trial. Following that incident, he attempted to go to a mosque in Dearborn, Michigan, a city that is home to one of the largest Muslim communities in the United States, and hold a prayer vigil on Good Friday of 2011. The point of that event was to discourage Muslims in that area of the country from seeking to impose sharia law (a conservative legal system set forth in the Qur'an) on the general population of that community. Court action was necessary to prevent that encounter from taking place.

People who hear about the activities of Terry Jones or the Westboro Baptist Church or the allegations involving Eddie Long are not likely to come away from those reports with a warm and trusting feeling about the church or clergy. Some people may stop to consider how small a group it is that is involved in these demonstrations. Others may simply see the images and hear the comments in the news media and decide to have nothing more to do with the church. These are the times in which effective pastoral care is being attempted by people whose lives are above reproach but whose profession is under suspicion.

The Failures of Some Must Not Deter the Best Efforts of Others
Despite the cloud of scandal and suspicion that hangs over the clergy these days, the challenge remains for us to serve our people with

integrity and humility. An even greater challenge may be to live and serve in such a way that we resist at every turn the invitations and temptations to join in the abuse of the pastoral office. We are not above doing such things; we are striving to keep the faith in what seems like an increasingly faithless generation. Perhaps we should join Isaiah who said: "Woe is me! I am lost, for I am a person of unclean lips and I live among a people of unclean lips." My slave ancestors put it well when they said:

> It ain't my mother,
> Or my father,
> But it's me, O Lord,
> Standing in the need of prayer.

Notes

1. Charles Wesley, "A Charge to Keep I Have," public domain.
2. For John Locke the good life was life, liberty, and the pursuit of property. Thomas Jefferson altered that last phrase in the Declaration of Independence to read life, liberty, and the pursuit of happiness.
3. Harry Emerson Fosdick, www.brainyquotes.com.
4. See Marvin A. McMickle, *Where Have All The Prophets Gone?* (Cleveland: Pilgrim, 2007); and Stephanie Y. Mitchem, *Name It and Claim It? Prosperity Preaching in the Black Church* (Cleveland: Pilgrim, 2007).
5. Stephen S. Smalley, *1, 2, 3 John*, Word Biblical Commentary (Waco, TX: Word, 1984), 346.
6. Smalley, 346.
7. Bruce Watson, *Freedom Summer* (New York: Viking Press, 2010).
8. Paul Vitello, *Taking a Break from the Lord's Work*, www.nytimes.com/2010/08/02/nyregion/02burnout.html, August 1, 2010, 1.
9. Vitello, 2.
10. Anne-Marie Hislop, letter to the editor, *New York Times*, August 15, 2010, Week in Review, 7.
11. G. Jeffrey MacDonald, "Congregations Gone Wild," *New York Times*, August 8, 2010, Sunday Opinion, 9.

CHAPTER 3

What Should the Church
Be Equipped to Do?

*"Whatever you did for one
of the least of these brothers
and sisters of mine,
you did for me."*
—Matthew 25:40 (NIV)

What is the work of the ministry for which the church needs to be built up by the pastors and teachers? We do not have to ponder this question as if the answer is not readily available. What Paul implies in Ephesians 4:11-13, Jesus spells out explicitly in Matthew 25:31-46. He says in verses 35-36: "I was hungry and you gave me food, I was thirsty and you gave me something to drink, I was a stranger and you welcomed me, I was naked and you gave me clothing, I was sick and you took care of me, I was in prison and you visited me." Each one of these categories points to an area of ministry in which pastors are involved on a regular basis. Pastoral care is not limited to pastoral counseling where the pastor sits with one or two people in an attempt to help them work through some personal problem. Jesus reminds us that pastoral care requires the church to reach out and touch the lives of people at the point of their greatest need and deepest despair.

Taking Direction from Ephesians 4 and Matthew 25

Ephesians 4:11-13 suggests that the central pastoral responsibility is to preach and teach in a way that equips believers to aggressively and consistently engage in the work of the ministry both within their local church and beyond.

Matthew 25:35-36 constitutes the lion's share of what the work of the ministry actually entails. And within the concentric circles model, it is these tasks to which the congregation is particularly called to partner in the work of ministry. There are, of course, other things in which pastors and congregations must be engaged that also represent different aspects of ministry. However, the specific areas mentioned in the Matthew passage should not be viewed as optional matters that believers can choose to embrace or ignore. These are things for which God will hold the church accountable on the Day of Judgment.

Jesus lifts up six specific areas in which pastoral care by both the pastor and an equipped congregation can be displayed. Four of those six areas of ministry offer some insight into how pastors can equip the church for the work of the ministry.

"I Was Hungry"— Pastors are frequently called on by people who do not know where their next meal will come from. Creating hunger centers and soup kitchens occupies the time of many pastors, especially in a time of record unemployment and increasing homelessness due to job losses followed by home foreclosures. Identifying and deploying volunteers who can assist with food collection and meal preparation and serving are necessary tasks. So is structuring the church budget in such a way that resources are systematically set aside to aid people inside and outside the church with emergency food relief.

We have people in our churches who never needed to go or gave any thought to going to a food pantry or a hunger center until they lost their jobs and suddenly were unable to feed themselves and their families. Today many such people stand in a food line with people they once may have served in the hunger center or ignored as they drove past. Churches must be equipped to share in ministry to the hungry. This problem is too big for the pastor to undertake alone. The congregation that has been equipped to do the work of the ministry will gladly find a way to be engaged in this area of human need.

"I Was Sick"— Pastors make an endless round of calls to hospitals, nursing homes, and hospice centers. There is, however, more to pastoral ministry to the sick than visiting people who are coping with traditional illnesses such as heart disease and cancer. Many pastors are called on to minister to persons infected with HIV/AIDS, a disease for which there is no cure. This requires a twofold approach to ministry—care for the infected that involves the people who carry the virus in their body, and care for the affected who are the families and friends who suffer with and care for those who are infected.[1]

From 1972 to 1976 I served on the staff of Abyssinian Baptist Church in New York City, a church that had members living in all five boroughs of New York City. When they were sick or hospitalized, my job was to go wherever they were to see about them. That was the first circle of pastoral care. On many occasions I would drive my car onto the Staten Island ferry and sail past the Statue of Liberty on my way to make a hospital call in that borough. As I walked into the room of one of our members in Staten Island, I could hear her telling someone on the phone that she was sure that no minister from her church would come all the way to Staten Island just to see about her. My mentor Samuel DeWitt Proctor made it clear to me that going to visit the sick was one of the most important things a minister can do. People who may quickly forget your sermons may never forget your presence or your prayers in their hospital room.

More work is involved in keeping up with the sick and shut-in list for the average church than the pastor can keep up with alone, which provides an opportunity for laypeople to get involved in caring for one another. This caring may include personal visits to hospitals, nursing homes, and hospice centers or the use of modern communications channels as a way to keep up with people who are sick. In addition to cards and letters that arrive through the postal service, no one should underestimate the power of e-mail and text messages and contact through Facebook and other social media. It is amazing to see what a caring Christian with computer skills can do in terms of showing care and concern for the sick.

"I Was a Stranger" — Throughout its history America has not been very kind to strangers. Whether Native Americans who lived here before the arrival of European settlers or people forcibly brought here from West Africa, those deemed to be strangers received horrific treatment in this country. This mistreatment of strangers was often done by Christians and in even more instances was done without any protest from the church. Other groups that have been viewed and treated as strangers in this country include the Chinese in California in the nineteenth century, Italians and Jews in the twentieth century, and the Hispanics who are attempting immigration into this country in the twenty-first century.

Many Americans, including some Christians, consider Muslims to be strangers. While Muslims are not newcomers to this country, they have taken on the status of strangers in the years since the terrorist attacks of September 11, 2001. Ten years after that event, the citizens of New York City and many other places across the country were up in arms about the idea of a mosque being built within a four-block proximity of Ground Zero (the site of the former World Trade Center towers). Many people have equated Islam with terrorism and all Muslims with Al Qaeda and the Taliban.[2] It is one thing when a journalist like Juan Williams of National Public

Radio gets fired for saying that he feels uncomfortable when he sees people dressed in Muslim garb. It is another matter altogether when Christian leaders and Christian churches respond to all Muslims with a similar sense of distrust and suspicion. That is because such criticism from Christian leaders may carry with it a level of authority and credibility on matters of religion not necessarily granted to journalists. As a result, Muslims in the United States remain one of the clearest examples of the stranger within our midst.

Pastors are being called into the fray to respond to a growing crisis as an anxious nation wrestles with whether the construction of new mosques should be allowed in their communities. Pastors have always been challenged to come to the aid of those whom others consider to be strangers, whether in the peaceful integration of a formerly all-white school or the acceptance of women into a field that many still believe to be an all-male enclave. The challenge is for the whole church to be equipped and trained to enter into such areas of ministry. This can mean being open and welcoming when people from within the group of strangers seek to join their congregation or move into their neighborhood or seek their vote for a political office.

"I Was in Prison"— Given the fact that more than two million people are housed in prisons and jails in the United States, it is not surprising that pastors are often involved in some form of prison ministry. Their ministry may involve leading a worship service inside a prison or hosting a support group in the church for returning ex-offenders. It may involve visiting adult facilities for men and women, and it might involve juvenile facilities for young people no more than twelve years old.

My first paid job in ministry was during my college years as a summer chaplain at the Illinois State Correctional School for Boys in St. Charles, Illinois, from 1968 to 1970. Ten years later while serving as a pastor in Montclair, New Jersey, I worked inside of the Ossining Correctional Facility of New York State (Sing Sing), made famous by movies in the 1940s featuring James Cagney and George Raft. I was part of the faculty of New York Theological Seminary that had received permission to offer a master of divinity degree to inmates who might become assistants to the prison chaplains. There are numerous prison ministry tasks in which pastors can be involved.

The challenge for pastors is to equip and encourage congregation members to share in prison ministry programs. As will be pointed out later in this book, 90 percent of the people who go into prisons in this country will be released back into the communities from which they came, and they will have many years of life left before them. Whether they become productive citizens or repeat offenders may well depend on whether people in local churches touch their lives both during and after their incarceration.[3]

A Biblical Model for Equipping the Saints

Because the work of the ministry cannot and should not be done solely by the senior pastor or even exclusively by the clergy, we need a workable model for pastors to equip believers to share in the ministry. Let me be clear: this is not a way for lazy pastors to avoid doing their job; it is a way to motivate sluggish congregations to begin doing the work God has called them to perform. Motivating church members to do the work of the church will not be easy, because too many Christians are perfectly content to "let the pastor do it." They may have to be pushed and persuaded to move outward from one circle to the next. But when the three concentric circles of pastoral care are employed, the church is being equipped, the body of Christ is being built up, and the work of the ministry is being accomplished by the whole church.

If churches do not begin to embrace such an approach to ministry, two unfortunate but inevitable outcomes will result. The first will be a burned-out and bummed-out group of clergy grown weary by their own work and frustrated by their inability to get the members of the congregation to share in much of anything beyond the Sunday morning worship service. The second unfortunate outcome will be the existence of a congregation of ministry onlookers who have been led to believe that they are consumer Christians whose only responsibility is to select from the menu of services offered by the pastor to meet their needs.

Once again, I propose a remedy for both of these possibilities: Ephesians 4:11-13 and the three concentric circles of pastoral care. Let us look briefly at each circle in turn.

Circle 1: A Caring Pastor— When I was serving a congregation in Montclair, New Jersey, between 1976 and 1986, one church family lived very near the church building. They had a daughter who once asked her parents, "What is Rev. McMickle's real job?" All she saw me doing was preaching on Sunday. I guess even a child could understand that the job of the pastor had to entail more than that.

The first circle involves the traditional understanding of pastoral care in which a caring and committed pastor ministers to the various needs of his or her flock. We will take a brief look at the pastor's various ministry tasks here and explore them further in chapter 6. As one might expect, caring for the flock involves the pastor engaged in the traditional areas of counseling, home and hospital visitation, preaching, performing weddings and funerals, and leadership in the priestly tasks of baptism and Communion. Many of these are tasks that occur largely within the context of the church building.

There are, however, many instances when a caring pastor displays pastoral care in ways that reach beyond the immediacy of congregational life and activity. Pastors may often find themselves writing letters of reference and recommendation for members as they interact with potential employers or college admissions offices.

Pastors may be called on to intercede for members as they seek assistance or information from social service or governmental agencies, including the Social Security Administration, the Veterans' Administration, and various divisions of the criminal justice system.

A caring pastor may even extend his or her ministry beyond the needs of the congregation and participate as a board member or a volunteer with some community group that delivers much-needed services to individuals and families. Groups ranging from the Red Cross to a local cancer support group, to the United Way, or to a grassroots HIV/AIDS ministry will often invite local pastors to serve on their boards or in one of their program areas. This allows pastors to extend their service into a wider sphere, and it also allows the agencies to broaden and diversify their representation within the community.

Circle 2: Caring Members— The second circle challenges pastors to see equipping the church to care for one another as chief among their duties. A careful study of Ephesians 4:11-13 reveals that ministry is not a spectator sport where a congregation watches while its clergy scurry around trying to save the world by themselves. That approach to ministry is reminiscent of a football game in which forty-five thousand people who badly need exercise sit and watch twenty-two people who badly need rest.

This idea of an active clergy and passive congregation is not accidental, even if it is inappropriate. As James Montgomery Boice points out, this dichotomy of activity may date back to the practices of the priesthood in ancient Israel when all of the sacrifices and rituals were performed by priests on behalf of the people. He further suggests that the Roman Catholic Church employed a similar approach to ministry, with priests performing the Mass, baptisms, last rites, and all the other seven core priestly functions while congregants observed and/or received. He even referenced the 1906 papal encyclical *Vehementer Nos*, which taught that members of the church "have no other duty than letting themselves be led, and of following their pastors as a docile flock."[4] Clearly, Ephesians 4:11-13 has a very different idea of how ministry should be conceived and accomplished; the clergy equip the church to do the work of the ministry rather than attempting to do all the work themselves.

Thomas Oden reinforces the approach to ministry in which the pastor equips the people to do the work of the ministry. He writes, "The pastor had best not do anything the body itself could do....The pastor's primary task is to equip the body, not try to do everything for the laity."[5]

Circle 3: A Caring (and Cared for) Community— The third circle of pastoral care may be the most difficult step for many pastors and congregations to make, but it may be the most Christlike action a local church can take. The third circle suggests that pastoral care occurs when the whole congregation has been equipped and encouraged to extend its care, concern, and compassion beyond its church membership to impact the people and problems that exist often just outside the front door of their local church. The challenge here is that some people might be inclined to view this third step as a form of community outreach or social activism that is best left to the church's social action committee. What the circles of care seek to do is make the congregation's care and concern for the people and problems within its immediate community a pastoral act, just as much as when the members within the congregation care for one another.

The work of the ministry is not simply the maintenance of a local church whose capacity for care and compassion reaches no further than its front door and the members who are already on the church rolls. Pastors are quite often involved as board members or volunteers with various community agencies and social service providers.

Congregations are usually content to let the pastor fill these roles without calling on them for any similar level of involvement. However, building up the body of Christ not only entails a strong fellowship inside the church, but also a caring and compassionate response to what resides beyond the walls of the church that is self-consciously done in the name of Jesus Christ.

Notes

1. Marvin A. McMickle, *A Time to Speak: How Black Pastors Can Respond to the HIV/AIDS Pandemic* (Cleveland: Pilgrim, 2008).

2. Eboo Patel, "Division vs. Unity," *USA Today*, August 30, 2010, A12.

3. *Ministry with Prisoners & Families: The Way Forward* by W. Wilson Goode Sr., Charles E. Lewis Jr., and Harold Dean Trulear (Valley Forge, PA: Judson Press, 2011) is a valuable resource for churches interested in prison ministry.

4. James Montgomery Boice, *Ephesians* (Grand Rapids: Baker, 1997), 140.

5. Thomas C. Oden, *Pastoral Theology* (New York: Harper&Row, 1983), 156.

CHAPTER 4

Pastoral Care Sits Just
Outside Our Doors

*"When you reap the harvest of your land, do not reap
to the very edges of your field or gather the gleanings of your
harvest. Do not go over your vineyard a second time or pick
the grapes that have fallen. Leave them for the poor and
the foreigner. I am the* LORD *your God."*
—Leviticus 19:9-10 (NIV)

While we will explore the third circle of pastoral care thoroughly
in chapter 10, it seems appropriate to build on the biblical foundation for this circle. After all, among the areas of pastoral care, this
has perhaps been considered "least of these" by the historic church.

The importance of a ministry that embraces the third circle of
pastoral care is helpfully illustrated by the story of the rich man
(Dives) and Lazarus in Luke 16:19-31. The story is about two men
who lived in close proximity of each other but nevertheless lived in
two very different worlds. One man is described as being dressed
in purple and linen, an indicator of his wealth and social status.
Another indicator of his wealth is his diet. We aren't told exactly
what he ate but that he "feasted sumptuously every day." His was
a life of luxury and excess. By contrast, we are introduced to a beggar named Lazarus who sat outside the rich man's house every day.

Despite his proximity to wealth and prosperity, Lazarus was covered in sores and "longed to satisfy his hunger with what fell from the rich man's table."

In verses 22-23 both men die and go to receive the reward for how they lived. The rich man goes to face torment in hell while Lazarus goes to a blessed reward in heaven. The question that must be considered is why the rich man goes to hell.

When I was a teenager during the days of the civil rights movement, this parable was often interpreted as being a racial paradigm in which the rich man was white and the poor man was black. It made us feel better to say that white people were going to hell because they did not respond to the plight of their poor black brothers and sisters who were waiting for justice just outside their doors.

Beyond Traditional Interpretations

As comforting as that interpretation was in the 1960s, it could not stand the simple test for faithful biblical interpretation that was passed on to me by my Old Testament professor James A. Sanders at Union Theological Seminary in New York City in the 1970s. He challenged us to remember that "whenever you read a portion of the Bible and you come away feeling better about yourself, you can be reasonably sure that you have just misread that portion of Scripture." We were challenged to keep reading until the words of Scripture were allowed to do their corrective work in our lives and not just in the lives of others.

With that lesson in mind, I returned to Luke 16:19-31 and discovered that no racial paradigm was involved since both men were likely members of the same Jewish community. What was at work was a class distinction that separated the man inside the house from the man seated just outside his door. The rich man did not go to hell because of his great wealth. To quote Harry Emerson Fosdick, the rich man went to hell because he was "rich in things but poor in soul."[1] The rich man was poor in terms of compassion for the poor man who suffered just outside his door every day.

The rich man could not enter and exit his own home without passing Lazarus. Probably multiple times every day he passed Lazarus without paying any attention to him or to his condition, or to what he might be able to do to alleviate Lazarus's desperate condition. The rich man assumed no personal responsibility for the people and problems just outside his door. That callous neglect allowed him to remain inside his house and enjoy his own prosperity without being moved by the poverty, sickness, and despair in the world around him. That blindness to his neighbor is what landed him in hell.

More Like the Rich Man Than Like Lazarus

One could argue that the church of Jesus Christ today behaves much more like the rich man on the inside of the house than it does like the poor man outside covered in sores and twisted with hunger. The church looks more like the man dressed in purple and linen who dines sumptuously every day than like the impoverished beggar whose torment is made worse by the dogs whose tongues transfer onto his open sores the bacteria they gather up with each trip to the trash heaps of that city. If this description of the church in the twenty-first century is true, then many churchgoing Christians can expect a fate similar to that of the rich man, which is to go straight to hell because they embraced a gospel of personal benefit and ignored or never heard a gospel of personal responsibility.

It is not enough for Christians to come to church on Sunday dressed in mink coats and designer clothes shouting to the tops of their lungs that they have been blessed by God. These conspicuous celebrations of prosperity on Sunday morning are no substitute for failing to notice Lazarus and the thousands like him who can be seen everywhere in our society. I have often thought about churchgoers and their sense of stewardship and discipleship in the following way. Some Christians wake up inside of $300,000 homes. They dress themselves in more than $3,000 of fashionable, even custom-made clothing. They drive to church in a $50,000 automobile. They take out a $200 Cross or Montblanc pen, with which they write a $10 check to support the work of the church. They then leave the church and drive to an upscale restaurant, content that they have given due attention to the state of their spiritual lives. Once they have dined "sumptuously," they leave as a tip for their server an amount that is very likely far greater than the amount they placed in the offering plate earlier that morning.

Can the Third Circle Keep Christians Out of Hell?

The challenge for pastors is to equip people for the work of the ministry that includes this third circle of care before it is too late. Many people in our churches think they have accomplished all that is expected of them when they attend church for an hour or two and make their nonsacrificial offering. This is not just a casual concern for today's church, and more than the future stability of the congregation is at stake. Lazarus sits outside the door of every church in one form or another, and pastors are responsible for equipping congregations to recognize and minister to the version of Lazarus that is nearest to them rather than acting as if their plight is entirely someone else's problem.

The third circle of pastoral care is meant to empower congregations to respond with love and generosity to the people and problems typified by Lazarus that reside within their sphere of influence. A failure to embrace this understanding of the gospel can result in a great portion of the churchgoing public ending up in hell next to the rich man from Luke 16 because, like him, they were never dislodged from their affinity for the gospel of personal benefit and challenged to embrace a gospel of personal responsibility for the real work of the ministry.

Surely that is what Jesus is saying to us after he set forth those areas of ministry in Matthew 25:31-46 in which the church must be involved. Jesus ends that passage by saying, "Just as you did not do it to the least of these, you did not do it to me. And these will go away into eternal punishment, but the righteous into eternal life." Attention to all three concentric circles of pastoral care can keep Christians from going to hell!

The Danger of an "Introverted Church"

James Harris is a seminary professor in the fields of preaching and pastoral theology at the Proctor School of Theology at Virginia Union University, as well as the senior minister of Second Baptist Church in Richmond, Virginia. From that dual vantage point, he has gained a theology of ministry that would likely not be possible for someone who occupied either of those roles separately. In his book *Pastoral Theology: A Black Church Perspective*, he describes the dangers of being a congregation that remains focused solely on its internal life and only on the needs of its members. He refers to such churches as being "introverted churches."[2] Other ways to describe such churches would be "insular" or "self-centered."

Borrowing from the work of Carl Jung who describes introverted personalities, Harris says that far too many churches evidence a similar set of characteristics. An introverted church is one that is subjective in its focus and action with little commitment to change or compulsion to address external stimuli. Harris extends his comments by saying, "The church acts like an independent entity, divorced from the suffering of the external world. It is basically silent, peaceful, and harmonious—failing miserably to understand the need to abandon its neutrality on issues of social and political justice...basking in the beauty of its bricks and mortar and the melodious syncretizing of its chancel choirs, pipe organs, and grand pianos."[3] Far too many churches approach ministry from this introverted model. As Harris points out, this approach "may contribute to numerical growth and internal excitement,"[4] but it fails to support that form of ministry that is inclined to extend its reach beyond its own walls and into the life and needs of the surrounding community.

What is needed, says Harris, is for the church to become an extroverted institution that will "move beyond personal conversion to community transformation."[5] To become an extroverted church, "the concept of community needs to be expanded to include the whole community—the church and the world. However, as long as the church is introverted and parochial in its approach to ministry, it will continue in its failure to effect liberation and change in the United States and the world."[6]

This idea of an extroverted institution is supported and even enriched by Rick Rusaw and Eric Swanson in their book *The Externally Focused Church*. They write, "It's not really church if it's not engaged in the life of the community through ministry and service."[7] They further contend that "God has placed churches in their communities (whether they feel wanted or not) to be salt, light, and leaven. They are not social workers but kingdom builders!"[8] The challenge of the pastor is the creation of a third circle of care in which the congregation willingly and faithfully reaches out to embrace and engage the people and problems that reside just outside the doors of their sanctuary. An "extroverted" or "externally focused" church is necessary if the ministry vision of Ephesians 4:11-13 is to be fulfilled.

In the next chapter, we will focus on the details involved in fulfilling the responsibilities of the first concentric circle—a caring pastor who properly shepherds the flock of God. I will attempt to give a fuller answer to the question that has haunted me for more than thirty-five years: "What is Rev. McMickle's real job?"

As I have attempted to answer that question for myself, I have developed an overarching vision of ministry that may be helpful to other pastors as well.

Notes

1. Harry Emerson Fosdick, "God of Grace and God of Glory," public domain.
2. James H. Harris, *Pastoral Theology: A Black Church Perspective* (Minneapolis: Fortress, 1991), 34–38.
3. Harris, 34–35.
4. Harris, 35.
5. Harris.
6. Harris, 36.
7. Rick Rusaw and Eric Swanson, *The Externally Focused Church* (Loveland, CO: Group, 2004), 24.
8. Rusaw and Swanson, 25.

Preliminary Questions for Consideration

1. Is your pastor externally focused, or is your pastor leading with an introverted or insular model?

2. Does your local church have an external focus, or is it preoccupied only with what goes on inside the walls of the church building?

3. Does the congregation respond positively when the pastor attempts to move them from being insular or introverted to being extroverted or externally focused?

4. Who are the people and what are the problems that reside just outside the doors of your church building?

5. Has Lazarus ever come and sat outside your door? Who was that person, and what did that person want?

6. Do you believe that Christians have any responsibility for responding to the social and economic problems that impact the lives of persons who do not belong to their local church?

7. Do the members of your local church give extravagantly to support the work of ministry?

8. What should the church do or say about Christians who are involved in a self-indulgent lifestyle?

9. How do you understand the words by Harry Emerson Fosdick that many Christians are "rich in things but poor in soul"?

10. What do you think will be said about you or about your church and your care for the poor and the needy when you stand before God in the final judgment?

The First Circle—
The Pastor as Shepherd

CHAPTER 5

Pastoral Care Begins with a Caring Pastor

"I will give you shepherds after my own heart,
who will feed you with knowledge and understanding."
—Jeremiah 3:15

In chapter 1 we identified pastoral care as an umbrella term that covers a vast array of ministry activities, many of which have traditionally been the responsibility of the pastor. Even in this model of all ministry as pastoral care, the reality of the pastor's work remains substantially unchanged. She or he remains the initiator, educator, and equipper of the congregation to share in the work of the ministry. Thus, this chapter will focus on the first circle of pastoral care, which is the way in which a caring pastor cares for the flock of God as the shepherd.

Remember Thomas Oden's exhortation to pastors to "learn properly to shepherd the flock of God"?[1] Remember as well the discussion of Isaiah 40:11 in chapter 1 and the idea that God will tend the flock like a shepherd? There I said that tending the flock like a shepherd does not refer to any one or two tasks that are performed by the shepherd on behalf of the flock. Instead, shepherding the flock of God includes all tasks associated with that role. A shepherd seeks to meet all the needs of the flock, from feeding and watering to protecting and occasionally having to discipline and correct. Tending the flock like a shepherd is not solely what pastors should be doing. Rather, the shepherding motif serves as the basis on which we can understand both why and how pastors should go about every ministry task they undertake, from counseling to preaching, to weddings and funerals, to church meetings and budget proposals. Through the use of this organizing principle, we establish the image of the pastor as a shepherd who serves out of a heart for God and God's people.

In chapter 6, I will give further attention to the various tasks and areas of interaction that constitute pastoral ministry and how the shepherding motif can and should inform how those tasks are performed. But before we turn to the "what" of pastoral care ministries, let us base our actions on a theory or philosophy of ministry that constitutes the "why" for the actions in which pastors engage.

An Ancient and Biblical Metaphor for Pastoral Ministry
In his book *The Christian Shepherd*, Seward Hiltner reminds us, "Shepherding is our most ancient metaphor for the tender and solicitous concern that the church and its ministers are to exercise to all persons in need. The actual work of shepherding has been known more often as pastoral care."[2] Hiltner reinforces the essential argument of this chapter, which is that shepherding (i.e., pastoral care) is not simply one task among many that is performed by the pastor. Hiltner says, "I think of shepherding as a perspective."[3] Shepherding is the overarching vision of ministry that informs pastors in all of the tasks they undertake as mentioned earlier by Thomas Oden. Pastors may be engaged in preaching, counseling, administration, visitation, leading a Bible study, or presiding over a Communion service. All of those tasks are part of the work of a pastor. They constitute what the pastor does in the context of properly shepherding the flock of God, what we are calling here the umbrella of pastoral (shepherding) care.

Timothy S. Laniak offers a biblical foundation to undergird the claims of Oden and Hiltner in his book, *Shepherds After My Own Heart: Pastoral Traditions and Leadership in the Bible.*[4] Laniak's thesis is that the Bible is full of the use of the shepherding metaphor, first as a way of describing how God has related to Israel and to the community of faith and, second, as the way of describing leaders within the faith community. Psalm 23 is one example of the former, declaring, "The LORD is my shepherd." Laniak observes that God consistently worked after the manner of ancient shepherds in dealing with Israel, providing them with provision, protection, and guidance.[5] Jeremiah 3:15 testifies to the latter use of shepherds in the Bible, by proclaiming the Lord's promise to provide Israel with shepherds after God's own heart.

Shepherd Leaders in Scripture: Moses and David — The two towering figures in the Old Testament are Moses and David, and both come to their positions of leadership out of a background as shepherds. Moses tended the sheep of Jethro until he was called on to shepherd God's people from slavery in Egypt to the Promised Land in Canaan. Moses was the instrument through which God shepherded Israel. Just before Moses died, he said to the Lord: "May the LORD, the God who gives breath to all living things, appoint someone over this community to go out and come in before them, one who will lead them out and bring them in, so the LORD's people will not be like sheep without a shepherd" (Numbers 27:16-17, NIV).

David tended the sheep of his father, Jesse, until he too was called to another task where those shepherding skills would come in handy—to be king of Israel, who was meant to serve the nation as a shepherd serves the flock. David is first introduced in the Bible when Samuel calls for the youngest son of Jesse, who was absent because he was "tending the sheep" (1 Samuel 16:11, NIV). Soon after Samuel anointed this shepherd boy to be the next king of Israel, David opposed and defeated the Philistine champion Goliath with his courage and a sling, the weapons of a shepherd (1 Samuel 17:34-37). Both Moses and David were called on to offer the three things expected of an ancient shepherd who cared for a flock: provision, protection, and guidance for the people God had placed under their care.

Adopting a Familiar Metaphor— In the New Testament, the shepherding motif continues. Jesus described himself as the Good Shepherd who lays down his life for the sheep (John 10:11-14). He also sent his apostles out as "shepherds to feed his sheep."[6] He sent the disciples as sheep among wolves (see Matthew 10:16) and later, after his resurrection, commissioned Peter with the repeated command, "Feed my sheep" (John 21:15-17).

Seward Hiltner reinforces the overarching argument of this entire book, namely, that "solicitous concern to all persons in need"[7] is not the sole responsibility of the minister or the clergy in the local church. That tasks, says Hiltner, belongs to "the church and its ministers." In that one simple statement, Hiltner provides theological and philosophical support for a ministry based on three concentric circles of pastoral care; the pastor may shepherd the flock, but the entire flock is called on to show "solicitous concern to all persons in need"—both inside and beyond the walls of the church.

Lessons from a Shepherd

The Shepherd Loves All the Sheep— It is interesting to note that there is no singular or plural distinction for the word *sheep*. A shepherd cares for the sheep whether that means one at a time or all of them together. As mentioned earlier, Isaiah 40:11 says this about God:

> He tends his flock like a shepherd:
> > He gathers the lambs in his arms
> and carries them close to his heart;
> > > he gently leads those that have young.
> > —Isaiah 40:11 (NIV)

God does not love the flock in general; God loves the sheep individually and according to their respective needs and conditions.

Jesus expands this idea in John 10:14-15 when he says about himself, "I am the good shepherd; I know my sheep and my sheep know me…and I lay down my life for the sheep" (NIV). Good shepherds care for all the members of the flock in whatever ways are rightfully required of them. Otherwise, says Jesus in verse 12, the person is nothing more than a "hired hand" who may work for pay but not out of love and commitment to the needs of the sheep.

Bear in mind that it may be difficult for some pastors to love "all" the sheep. The pastor may encounter some people in a given congregation with a sense of dread. Maybe such persons are openly critical of everything the pastor says or does. Maybe they are living or behaving in ways in which the pastor, and perhaps the Scriptures, are not supportive. Maybe they require attention from the pastor, but they were vocal in supporting a different pastoral candidate during the search process. All of that notwithstanding, Jesus calls pastors to follow his example of loving "all" the sheep in the flock.

Pastors who serve as shepherds should be careful not to play favorites and respond to certain members above others. Church officers and leaders should not expect their position in the church to grant them more or priority access to the pastor above those who hold no position or who do not give as much financial support to the church. There may be people in every congregation who feel the cold shoulder from some members of that church for one reason or another. Maybe they are single parents, persons infected with HIV/AIDS, persons in the lesbian/gay/bisexual/transgender community, or foreign-born people who do not have a good grasp of the English language. There are many more reasons why certain people may not feel welcome in some churches. Pastors who serve as shepherds should be especially careful to rise above any of these petty prejudices or beliefs. This is the difference between good shepherds who love the sheep and "hired hands" who work at a church for a living but do not want to be bothered with certain people.

A second aspect to being a good shepherd involves not only loving all the sheep, but also loving or at least seeking to be proficient at all aspects of the job of shepherding. Unfortunately, some pastors make decisions about what tasks they will and will not perform based solely on personal preferences. For example, those who like to preach may devote hours to the task of sermon preparation, but if they do not like to make sick and hospital calls, they will simply leave that task undone. Those who like interacting with older people will be available for anything that involves that part of the congregation. But if they do not enjoy being around young people, they will always be unavailable to that group no matter what the need may be. This is not how a good shepherd cares for the flock.

A great many tasks may be required of a pastor that he or she does not enjoy as much as some other tasks, but they must be done nonetheless! The pastor may enjoy being with certain groups within the church or community more than others. But it may be the persons the pastor least enjoys being around that may be most in need of the shepherd's care and concern. This is part of what is involved in learning properly to shepherd the flock of God.

A Shepherd Serves the Flock— When a pastor operates from a shepherding perspective, he or she is committing to care for and even make sacrifices on behalf of the flock. I am deeply concerned about a trend in church life in which pastors think that ministry is primarily a matter of being taken care of by the congregation rather than the other way around. Proper pastoral care involves a willingness to place the well-being of the flock uppermost in one's mind. Jesus made that clear in John 10 in his discussion of what constitutes a "good shepherd." He said, "The thief comes only to steal and kill and destroy....I am the good shepherd. The good shepherd lays down his life for the sheep" (John 10:10-11, NIV). Granted that in this "I am" saying, Jesus is focusing on himself and his love and care for those who follow after him. Nevertheless, he serves as a model of how pastors should serve as shepherds of God's flock, to care for the flock and not to fleece it for any personal gain.

It is disheartening to encounter pastors who believe that they have no other responsibility toward the flock of God than to preach a sermon on Sunday. At the same time, they fully expect the congregation to provide them with a level of luxurious living that greatly exceeds anything most members of the congregation could ever afford for themselves.

Imagine the statement that is being made when a Bentley automobile or its equivalent is parked outside an inner-city church where the membership is battling with unemployment, home foreclosure, crushing debt, and uninsured medical expenses. Those whose ministry is informed by the philosophy of prosperity theology may not see any problem with this scenario. Those who feel themselves called to serve the flock of God may see such self-indulgence as contradictory to their ministry and to the gospel message!

A Shepherd Remains True to That Vocation— Operating from a shepherding perspective may also aid pastors in deciding when, where, and how they will invest their time, talent, and training. They may consider some tasks inappropriate. All pastors would likely agree to a request to lead a Bible study, whether held inside the church or in some community setting. On the other hand, many pastors might say no to a request to offer a prayer at a political rally where explicit instructions have been given about *not* mentioning the name of Jesus. Anyone who feels a primary calling to feed the flock of God need not accept such an assignment.

Pastors do not have to honor requests simply because they have been made. Civic and political involvement can be important and rewarding tasks for those engaged in pastoral ministry, but those involvements often come cloaked in subtle temptations that can seduce pastors who are more interested in the accolades of politicians and civic leaders than in hearing "Well done" from God. So many requests for the pastor's time may be made that fulfilling all of the responsibilities of his or her office becomes difficult. How much time should be made available for clergy associations, denominational involvements, ecumenical and interfaith activities, and invitations to preach or teach at other churches or conferences in one's community or within a broader sphere of involvement? At what point does the flock begin to suffer due to the persistent absence of the shepherd in their midst? I know many pastors who boast about being away from their flock up to thirty-five weeks each year while they preach revivals across the country. That may be enriching for the shepherd, but one is left to wonder about the flock that must spend so much time without the shepherd being among them.

Time set aside for working beyond the life of one's flock is not the only issue of time management that pastors must consider. They must also ask themselves the following: How much time am I setting aside for personal spiritual formation? How much time am I setting aside for continuing education and professional enrichment? How much time am I setting aside for my family life, spouse, and children? Can I be effective if I am constantly drained physically, unsatisfied with my home life, and not stimulated by regular reading and reflection?

A Shepherd Learns How to Minister in a Multifaith World— A pastor must also consider whether to involve the local church in ecumenical conversations among Christian groups that hold the name of Jesus in common, or in interfaith or multifaith activities designed to bring together persons of various religious traditions— Christian, Jewish, Muslim, Buddhist, Hindu, and others. Much can be gained by interreligious dialogue, but it is helpful to have a philosophy of ministry that guides whether a pastor should or should not embrace such activities. When it comes to interfaith (two major religious traditions of the world) and multifaith (three or more world religions engaging one another) programs, some believe that John 14:6—"I am the way and the truth and the life. No one comes to the Father except through me" (NIV)—prohibits such activities. But the issue cannot be escaped that easily, because in the twenty-first century, interfaith and multifaith encounters are much more likely to occur than ever before in the history of the church in the United States. When I was in seminary (1970–73), Christians were shocked when a Presbyterian married a Pentecostal. Today it is just as likely that a Baptist might choose to marry a Buddhist. Christian pastors who operate from a shepherding perspective will have to decide how to respond when a member of their congregation announces their intention to marry someone of another faith tradition.

A good shepherd will want to meet with the couple and counsel them on the challenges that may await them as an interfaith couple. Similarly, a good shepherd may need to meet with the families of the couple and help them think through any initial concerns about an interfaith marriage. A caring pastor may urge the couple to give some attention to the warning by Paul about being unequally yoked (2 Corinthians 6:14) as that Scripture relates to the dynamics involved when a Christian marries someone of another faith tradition or of no religious tradition at all. This does not necessarily mean that the two people should not get married, but it does mean there are some aspects of the Christian faith that will need to be considered as part of the premarital counseling process.

Finally, a caring pastor will have to decide whether to preside over or participate in an interfaith wedding. Each pastor must decide whether the truly caring thing to do is to counsel against such a marriage and refrain from any participation in it or to support the couple in their decision and provide them with as much counsel and support as possible. The decision of a pastor not to participate in an interfaith wedding does not mean that the couple in question will choose not to get married. Instead, they may go to a secular authority qualified to preside over marriages. Each pastor must decide for himself or herself what is the most caring way to proceed in such an instance.

How the pastor responds when asked to preside at such a wedding will be based either on the pastor's feelings at the moment or on a clearly articulated philosophy of ministry that allows the pastor to say yes or no based on clearly defined and deeply held principles. Would a Christian pastor participate in a non-Christian ceremony held in a synagogue or mosque? Would a Christian pastor allow a rabbi or imam to participate in their own faith tradition in a ceremony held in the church? Such questions are not mere speculations involving unlikely scenarios; these remind me of the warning from Geddes Hanson, one of my mentors at Princeton Theological Seminary in the 1980s, about thinking in advance about what will happen sooner or later.

Practice of Ministry Must Be Informed by a Theory of Ministry

How does a pastor know when it is necessary to say yes to some requests, but at the same time have a well-grounded reason for saying no to some other requests from people who might be seeking the pastor's time and attention? Most seasoned pastors already know, and those pastors who are just starting out in ministry will soon discover, that the opportunity always exists to be involved with more and more tasks both inside the church and beyond.

At some point, pastors need to learn how to say no to some requests for their involvement. But on what basis do they make the determination of the things to which they will and will not commit themselves? Ray S. Anderson speaks to this very point when he writes, "The primary purpose of practical theology is to ensure that the church's public proclamation and praxis in the world faithfully reflects the nature and purpose of God's continuing mission to the world, and in so doing authentically addresses the contemporary context into which the church seeks to minister."[8] So one way pastors can decide whether to involve themselves in one task over against another is by asking how involvement in this task "faithfully reflects the nature and purpose of God's continuing mission to the world." That reference to practical theology is an appeal to a theory of ministry that can help pastors determine how to accept, reject, or prioritize the many requests for a pastor's attention that come every day. Perhaps there is wisdom for pastors in a line from Shakespeare's *Hamlet*, in which a loving father offers advice to his son who is about to leave their home in a small village and venture off to the great city of Paris. Knowing all the temptations that could await his son there, the father offers these words of wisdom: "This above all else: to thine own self be true."

To every pastor who feels twisted and pulled in multiple directions, and who may also be inclined to embrace only part of the work or to love only a portion of the flock, the advice being given here is closely aligned with the words of Shakespeare: This above all else: be true to the full understanding of what it means to be a pastor operating with the motif of a shepherd!

Notes

1. Thomas C. Oden, *Pastoral Theology* (New York: Harper&Row, 1983), 13.
2. Seward Hiltner, *The Christian Shepherd: Some Aspects of Pastoral Care* (Nashville: Abingdon, 1959), 7.
3. Hiltner, 14.
4. Timothy S. Laniak, *Shepherds After My Own Heart: Pastoral Traditions and Leadership in the Bible* (Downers Grove: InterVarsity, 2006).
5. Laniak, 80–87.
6. Laniak, 23.
7. Hiltner, 7.
8. Ray S. Anderson, *The Shape of Practical Theology: Empowering Ministry with Theological Praxis* (Downers Grove, IL: InterVarsity, 2001), 22.

CHAPTER 6

Pastoral Care in All Pastoral Ministry

I am the Good Shepherd; I know my sheep and my sheep know me.
—John 10:14

This book explains pastoral care in a way that is decidedly different from traditional thinking. Generally the church has considered pastoral care to be a separate and distinct ministry task alongside preaching, leading worship, facilitating group dynamics, administering church business, and so on. Because the concentric circles paradigm conceives of pastoral care (i.e., shepherding) as the overarching perspective under which all ministry is approached, the specific ministry tasks to be considered in this chapter will be viewed through a lens of pastoral care. It is because we care for the people of God that we preach, pray, visit, comfort, console, preside at weddings and funerals, perform baptisms and christenings, and represent and advocate for the sheep in places far beyond the walls of the local church. Pastoral care is not merely what we do as pastors; it is the heart of who we are and why we serve.

Tasks Involved in the First Circle of Pastoral Care
We have learned that the first circle of pastoral care involves a caring and concerned pastor acting as the shepherd of the flock and

nurturing and sustaining the faith of those under his or her care. In this role, the pastor will devote much time and attention to a variety of tasks. In most cases, those tasks will not result in any dispute from the clergy or the laity. The pastor may lead in the service of baptism or in the dedication of infants. The pastor may plan for and preside over funeral services. The pastor may visit people in prison and preach to an assembly that includes inmates and prison staff together. The pastor may attend a weekend retreat with the youth group or an afternoon luncheon with the seniors ministry. The pastor may represent the congregation on denominational committees or on the board of local civic and cultural organizations.

Many books offer valuable insights into the nature and scope of the work of the pastor. I heartily commend *We Have This Ministry: The Heart of the Pastor's Vocation* by two of my mentors in ministry, Samuel D. Proctor and Gardner C. Taylor.[1] They outline a list of seven areas that touch on aspects of the pastor's vocation. They include the pastor as teacher, counselor, intercessor, and administrator. They also touch on the pastor's role in times of crisis in the family, the pastor who works within the broader public forums of the community to help shape consensus or at least understanding on matters of public policy. Finally they consider who gets directly involved in politics, whether as a candidate or as an active supporter of candidates who might serve in ways that benefit God's people or work to support values the pastor perceives to be consistent with the kingdom of God.

What should not go unnoticed is that Proctor and Taylor do not begin with a listing of the tasks that are to be done. Instead, it begins with a discussion of the preacher's call and points to the fact that the tasks are to be performed by someone who is operating out of a specific perspective. Pastoral work in all of its forms is a calling from God to serve God's people and in the end to be accountable to God for the way the pastor has gone about the work. Thus, Proctor and Taylor do not begin their book with a long list of "what to do"; they begin with a clear focus on *who* performs these tasks and *why* they are engaged in those tasks to begin with.

A time may come in one's ministry when the performance of the various tasks of pastoral care will seem to be ineffective and unproductive. The pastor may become discouraged when the congregation does not seem to be growing either in number or in maturity. A time may come when a pastor may think about quitting the ministry in favor of some more "highly favored" and financially rewarding vocation that does not have attached to it the 24/7 demands of ministry by which congregation members may reach out to the pastor without apology at any time of day and on any day of the week.

How a person carries that reality through life very much depends on who they understand themselves to be as pastor. If they see themselves as being called by God properly to shepherd the flock of God, then they might not protest too much when it is time to leave the ninety-nine sheep safely in the fold and go after the one sheep that has gotten lost in the wilderness. True enough, parameters must be set that will allow for pastoral self-care and for secure times when the pastor can be personally nurtured by time with his or her own family. However, those personal and vocational parameters will be informed by each pastor's understanding of who he or she is called to be by God and among the people of God. What I am arguing here and what Proctor and Taylor place foremost in their book is that the daily practice of ministry is informed by the underlying and overarching philosophy of ministry that guides pastors in the performance of their duties over the course of a lifetime in ministry. And in this paradigm, the theory of ministry is rooted in the biblical metaphor of the shepherd.

Additional Resources for Defining the Tasks of Pastoral Care

I wish to recommend two other books that offer a useful overview of tasks that rightfully occupy the time of those engaged in pastoral ministry. One is *Perfecting the Pastor's Art* by C. Avery Lee and Gardner C. Taylor.[2] They highlight preaching, including time for rigorous study and theological reflection in sermon preparation, the demands of church administration, especially as it relates to how effective organizations can best serve the needs of the members, and the performance of weddings and funerals, offering a priestly presence at critical times of transition and intense emotions. All of these are activities familiar to clergy in the first circle of pastoral care. Lee and Taylor also add the urgency of pastoral self-care to the responsibilities of pastoral leaders.

A second book that bears consideration when thinking about the tasks involved in properly shepherding the flock of God is *The Work of the Pastor* by Victor D. Lehman.[3] Allowing for the overlap that is likely to occur when people look to define the major areas of pastoral ministry, Lehman brings some additional pastoral tasks into focus beyond those mentioned by Lee, Proctor, and Taylor. He begins with the work of the pastor as leader in the worship service and looks at the sermon that is delivered in that context. He then lists pastoral care as a category unto itself, and under that heading he mentions such specific tasks as crisis care, visitation, counseling, and care for those who might best be described as "special needs" people in the congregation. His list concludes with conflict management; maintaining a team ministry in which duties are shared among the pastoral staff and volunteers; church administration; and finally the duties associated with denominational, ecumenical, and even interfaith collaborations.

The book by Lee and Taylor also lists the tasks of ministry after it has dealt with the pastor's call and the sense of vocation. As in Proctor and Taylor's book, these authors remind us that the most important thing in pastoral ministry is not the list of "what to do" but rather a clear sense about why and how one is doing a certain task. There are inevitably aspects of pastoral ministry, ranging from sick visits and hospital calls to church administration that a pastor might not enjoy. However, it is an overarching sense of vocation anchored in the call from God that sustained clergy even when called on to do things we did not enjoy but which we know are beneficial to caring properly for the flock of God.

Forms of Pastoral Care

Now let's look briefly at how shepherding informs four essential areas of pastoral care: visitation of the sick, preaching and worship, church administration, and officiating in the ordinances of baptism and Communion. I will direct a few paragraphs toward each of these forms of pastoral ministry to bolster the central claim of this book that pastoral care is not merely a list of tasks to be done, but is the shepherding perspective from which all pastoral work is performed.

Visiting with the Sick— Gardner C. Taylor once said, "One of the things I did not look forward to was visitation....I could find a thousand things to do in my office to delay my visiting." He went on to say, however, "Ironically, once I went, I would find these visits to be among the most rewarding parts of my ministry."[4] He later pointed to why those sick visits were important when the task was viewed from the shepherding perspective as an approach to ministry. In speaking to successive generations of pastors Avery Lee said, "Young pastors ought to remember that they are in the pastorate largely because of a concern for people. This includes people who are sick and in hospitals. Even if nothing can be said or done, just a visit from the pastor can be very uplifting. It shows that you care. Pastors should never underestimate what this means to people."[5]

These words from Lee and Taylor call to mind an approach to ministry that was drilled into me by Samuel Proctor when I served on the pastoral staff at Abyssinian Baptist Church in New York City between 1972 and 1976. Dr. Proctor served there as the senior pastor from 1972 to 1989, but during that time he remained involved with teaching as the Martin Luther King Jr. Professor at the Rutgers University School of Education. One of the ways he handled those dual responsibilities was by sharing some of the pastoral load with his staff ministers. Bear in mind that the congregation exceeded two thousand persons living in all five boroughs of New York City, as well as in parts of New Jersey and Connecticut.

While Dr. Proctor always visited as many members of the church as possible, he understood that he could not cover all of that territory alone, even if he had no other duties or responsibilities. Therefore, he expected us to take on a fair share of the ministry of visitation in homes and in hospitals. I can hear him telling me over and over again that most people will forget what you might have said within moments of having heard any given sermon. But what they will likely never forget is the day you walked into their hospital room before or after surgery and had prayer with them. That level of concern for the flock, no matter how large or far-flung it might be, is at the heart of the shepherding perspective by which what you do is informed by who you believe yourself to be!

When the shepherding motif informs a visit in a hospital, nursing home, hospice center, prison visitation area, or church member's home, one rule should inform the pastor above all else: take time to visit. Rushing in and out of the room where the visit is occurring may serve the scheduling needs of a busy pastor, but it does not really conform to the idea of "feeding the flock like a shepherd."

Take the time to visit—to listen to what the person may want to say or share—and to read Scripture and pray. Take the time even for small talk about any news of the day that may help lift the person's thoughts beyond his or her immediate circumstances and/or condition. Ask about any upcoming tests or procedures the person may want to discuss with you. Inquire about other members of the family if there are any who might be impacted by what is happening in the life of the person with whom you are visiting. Do not be distracted by your technology. Sending text messages and reading e-mails can wait until the visit is over. Pastoral visits can become sacred time when the pastor goes about that task with the motif of being a good shepherd at the center of his or her perspective.

Preaching and Worship— Sunday mornings may be the only time when the pastor will encounter the majority of the members of the flock. That being the case, everything that happens that day should be approached from a shepherding perspective. Sermon selection and the format and design of worship services become wonderful opportunities to care for the flock. I have been helped by Cleophus Larue, who suggests that preaching themes and subjects can be rotated to include such areas as personal piety, care of the soul, social justice, corporate (community) concerns, and the maintenance of the institutional church.[6] Such an approach or some personal variation of these suggested topics allows for a careful and consistent feeding of the flock.

It is important to remember that there are many more opportunities for pastoral care during a worship service than delivering sermons. The selection of hymns at various points during the service should be strategic—before the pastoral prayer, in response to the preached Word, during an altar call, and even when the tithes and offerings are being gathered. Obviously, every worship service is punctuated by prayer—invocation, offertory, pastoral, intercessory, and benediction. Each one of those prayers should be viewed as an opportunity for pastoral care.

Church Administration— The day-to-day operation of a church should definitely be approached from the perspective of pastoral care. What principles will inform the creation and oversight of a church budget? By what screening process will employees and lay leaders be selected? What rules will regulate how and when church-owned facilities—from the church van to the copy machine, to the kitchen and other spaces in the building—can be used? What policies will govern how funerals should be conducted if held in the church sanctuary? Does the church already have a constitution or by-laws? When should they be updated to provide ongoing structure for the corporate life of the institution?

A person operating with a heart for pastoral care will not use the office of the pastor as a tool with which to bully or exploit people or as an occasion to use any perceived power as a means for personal gain. Instead, using the language of Paul, a caring pastor simply wants to be sure that things are done "decently and in order" (1 Corinthians 14:40).

As is set forth in my book *Deacons in Today's Black Baptist Church*, one of the best illustrations of pastoral care employed with a shepherd's heart is found in Acts 6 where a problem exists regarding the equitable distribution of the commonly held resources of the first-century church in Jerusalem. Widows of Greek-speaking converts to the Christian faith brought their concerns to the twelve apostles in the hope that they would correct an issue of blatant ethnic or cultural discrimination. Peter offered a masterful blending of administrative skill and pastoral care when he directed that seven persons fitting a specific profile should be selected from within the community. Those seven persons would be ordained by the apostles and given responsibility for carrying out that area of ministry.[7] Pastors should learn from Peter how to engage in church administration with a shepherd's heart.

The Ordinances of the Church— By the use of the word *ordinances*, my Baptist heritage is emerging. Without fighting over the use of the words and concepts of ordinances versus sacraments, let me simply point to pastoral care during baptism and Holy Communion. Clearly, other groups might be inclined to extend the list at this point to include weddings and funerals. I will speak to those things as well, but not under the heading of ordinances or sacraments. Those are simply two other occasions for pastoral care by a caring shepherd.

The pastoral care involved in the ordinance of baptism is more than the act of baptizing someone into the faith in accordance with Matthew 28:19-20. Teaching to introduce people to the reasons for baptism and the theology that undergirds it (i.e., as in Romans 6:3-4 where baptism is portrayed as a person's being buried with Christ and then raised into newness of life) should take place before baptism. For those who practice believer's baptism in which a personal confession of faith precedes baptism, this teaching occurs before a candidate is baptized. For those who practice infant baptism, this teaching occurs later, most likely during a confirmation class.

After forty years in pastoral ministry, I still find myself transfixed when I stand behind the Communion table. This is when pastors can remind the faithful that while salvation may be free for the believer, it was purchased by the blood and suffering of Jesus Christ. The Lord's Supper, Holy Communion, the Eucharist, or the Mass for Roman Catholics is a sacred time. The meaning of the elements should be explained. The reasons why we take Communion should be reiterated. The central role of the cross in Christian theology should be emphasized. Music appropriate for the occasion should be selected to be sung or played. Even as I write these words I find myself singing:

> How marvelous the grace that caught my falling soul;
> He looked beyond my faults and saw my need.[8]

Pastoral Counseling— The most delicate issue to be resolved in this book is the interface between traditional understandings of pastoral care and pastoral counseling. Some pastors may be operating with an understanding of pastoral care that is synonymous with and extends no further than pastoral counseling. That is to say, their understanding of what it means to engage in pastoral care is to sit in the church office and offer compassion, concern, and counsel to members of the congregation who seek out the pastor for that purpose. Some pastors approach their sense of vocation from the perspective of a clinician who is offering some form of professional counseling. Of course pastors who operate from the shepherding perspective will be involved in pastoral counseling from time to time. The concern being raised here involves those instances when pastoral counseling becomes the sum total of pastoral care, with no time or attention being directed to the full implications of the three circles of pastoral care. As I have argued with all of the ministry tasks discussed earlier in this chapter, pastoral counseling is not another name for pastoral care. Pastoral counseling should be approached from the perspective that all ministry tasks should be seen as opportunities for pastoral care.

For some persons, the phrase *pastoral care and counseling* suggests an entire field of theological and professional study unto itself. In *Biblical Themes for Pastoral Care*, William B. Oglesby Jr. says, "It goes without saying that the importance of pastoral care and counseling has been recognized by the church from the beginning....The crucial question turns on how it should be done."[9] That is indeed the question, and the answer in this book is to unlink those two terms so as to allow pastoral counseling to become one of many skills that falls under the broad category of pastoral care. This does not minimize pastoral counseling in any way; it simply suggests that when one operates under the shepherding perspective as one's theory of ministry, pastoral counseling is but one of the many things that a shepherd does in the process of properly caring for the flock of God.

Because pastoral counseling is one of the forms of pastoral care, pastors should make themselves as proficient as possible when it comes to this particular task. For many people, seeking pastoral counsel from their local church is a first step on the road to finding answers, solutions, or needed assistance. The pastor may not be able to resolve the problem but may be able to offer an initial diagnosis and direction that can result in a solution.

For some, pastoral counseling becomes a specialized call to a particular kind of licensed and credentialed ministry. That is the case for one of my colleagues at Ashland Theological Seminary, professor of pastoral counseling Dr. David Mann. He states unashamedly that he was called to the ministry but not necessarily to ministry that involved preaching or serving as pastor of a congregation. Those who answer the call to a ministry of pastoral counseling are in no sense less engaged in ministry than those who serve as "real pastors." Many seminaries now offer robust programs in pastoral counseling. Some programs prepare the graduate for licensing by the state, which allows the credentialed counselor to offer professional services for a fee. Many churches are opening or sponsoring counseling centers that serve church members and people from the community. These ministries are especially effective when conducted by fully trained and licensed professionals.

The church needs such professionally trained counselors who bring together the best of biblical and theological reflection with the best in behavioral studies—particularly when it comes to circumstances that require longer-term counseling and more specialized therapy. Thus, part of the ministry of pastoral care that is integral to the task of pastoral counseling is the discernment of when the local pastor should refer a parishioner to a licensed pastoral counselor, therapist, or recovery program. Indeed, part of the good shepherd's responsibility is to maintain an up-to-date data base of colleagues in other fields to whom the shepherd can turn when faced with something that exceeds his or her own capacities to address.

The Ministry of Presence— In addition to all of the tasks that have been listed thus far, there is one more way by which pastors show care and concern for the flock of God: the ministry of presence.

The mere presence of the shepherd in the midst of the flock is reassuring to those under the shepherd's supervision. The presence of the pastor also serves as a source of comfort and encouragement to members of the flock of God, especially during times of crisis like sickness or death. At times there are simply no words to say. In fact, sometimes words just get in the way. There is, however, great power in the mere presence of the pastor in a hospital room where someone is awaiting surgery, in a home after someone has died, at the scene of an accident where someone has been seriously injured, or in a Red Cross shelter after a fire has destroyed a home.

To be sure, there are times when the pastor should be ready and willing to speak or act as he or she has been trained to do as the means by which care and comfort are exhibited. But at other times nothing can be said, at least not at a certain moment, that can be as helpful as simply showing up and being present as a sign of care and concern. I can recall as though it were yesterday when the daughter of two of our members at Antioch died in a plane crash. An intense fire at the crash site had consumed everything and everybody on board the plane. Nothing of their daughter could be recovered. Nothing could be placed in a coffin or an urn for burial.

When I went to their home upon hearing this news I did not walk in and begin offering them some reassurance about eternal life for their daughter or about "precious memories" for them. I held them and hugged them and let them cry on my shoulder. I sat with them while others in the congregation came by to offer their condolences. My presence was not really about me; it was about what the presence of a pastor unleashes in the heart and mind of a believer. The presence of the pastor is a reminder that those who grieve do not have to do so alone, a reminder of the promises of Scripture that people can cling to in times of crisis, a reminder that God is with God's people at all times and in all places. I would have plenty of time for words—in prayer, in the reading of Scripture, and in a eulogy. What is often needed is the shepherd's presence.

In *The Authentic Pastor*, Gene Bartlett examined the ministry of presence. He said, "As the physician represents forces of healing that are outside himself or herself, so the pastor represents the transcendent powers to which we reach out in times of need." He added, "The minister represents that to which we reach out, not in himself or herself alone, but in the very faith for which the minister stands." Bartlett suggested that there is a "representative nature to the pastoral practice that is surprising in its effect."[10] The power, the comfort, and the reassurance that are available are not simply because the pastor is in the room or on the scene. What is really at work is the activation of all the resources of faith and hope the pastor "represents" in the lives of members of the flock with whom he or she has had a preexisting relationship.

We claim this in our relationship with God who is our shepherd. The psalmist David wrote, "Even though I walk through the darkest valley, I will fear no evil, for you are with me; your rod and your staff, they comfort me" (Psalm 23:4, NIV). The power of this passage is not in anything the shepherd actually says or does. The power is in the shepherd's presence with the sheep in the darkest valley. To a lesser degree, but in the same spirit, comfort comes from the knowledge that the pastor is here with us. That is why, even after a body has been committed at the cemetery and my official duties are complete, I remain standing for several minutes at the head of the grave. I am not saying or doing anything. I am, by standing at that spot at that moment, representing the promise of God that death does not have the last word for the one we have just buried, and God is able to comfort those who grieve the loss.

Pastoral Functions in Pastoral Care

Pastors should be familiar with what are known as the "four pastoral functions of *healing, guiding, sustaining,* and *reconciling.*"[11] In essence, that concept suggests that some problems and conditions can be *healed*, resolved once and for all. In other cases, people need to be *guided*, directed to other sources that can aid in eventual resolution. In still other instances, no solution is yet in sight, and people need to be *sustained* and encouraged until help arrives. *Reconciling* happens only when relationships with God or with each other have been resolved through an act of forgiveness.

Consider the various ways by which these four approaches to pastoral care can occur in the life of any local church. Pastors can aid persons through the healing process not only as they recover from physical sickness, but also as they recover from divorce, the death of a loved one, a frayed relationship, or the lingering problem of not being able to forgive themselves for something even though God may already have done so.

Pastors are guiding people all the time as they aid them in finding employment, seeking the expungement of a criminal record, or finding meaning in life when marriage or any other permanent relationship seems not to be on the horizon. Sustaining occurs when pastors comfort and console persons who have loved ones who have been deployed by the armed forces into a war zone or sentenced by a criminal court to a prison term.

Reconciling can occur as part of the preaching and teaching ministry of the church as persons are urged to embrace the idea in 2 Corinthians 5:17-21 that God in Christ reconciled the world to himself and gave us the ministry of reconciliation. Pastors can facilitate reconciliation between members of groups within the church that seem to be at odds over a matter of church practice or policy. Obviously, a pastor who does not hold grudges and does not seek to facilitate disunity by his or her own actions is essential if the ministry of reconciliation is to be embraced as an aspect of pastoral care.

Shepherds Require Training to Fulfill Their Role

I was profoundly moved by a comment from author and pastor Paul Nixon. He said, "I graduated from seminary in 1986, ready for ministry in 1976. The how-to's are changing in pastoral ministry, faster in my lifetime than perhaps ever before."[12] To be sure, some aspects of theological education are timeless and relevant from generation to generation—the techniques of biblical exegesis, the study of Reformation history, even the introduction to the great creeds and doctrines of the Christian faith in general and of various denominations and movements in particular. However, the skills and techniques for doing pastoral ministry are matters that must be taught with a keen awareness of the times and places in which persons are going forth to serve.

Regrettably, too many things taught in seminary may have nothing at all to do with being equipped to be an effective pastor and shepherd. In fact, I am convinced that some seminaries and divinity schools have no interest whatsoever in helping men and women learn properly to shepherd the flock of God. They seem more focused on producing scholars than on equipping people to be pastors. When I was a seminary student, the seminary catalog suggested that part of the mission of the school was to produce "scholarly pastors." My recollection of those years is that far more emphasis was placed on the scholarly component than on anything having to do with being a pastor.

Much of what I learned about being a pastor came from my field work setting and my later employment at Abyssinian Baptist Church in New York City under Samuel DeWitt Proctor. I recall how many friends of mine at other seminaries declared that they learned more about being a pastor in the living room of a local pastor than they did in any class at school. However it is done, pastors have to move beyond the core curriculum of a seminary, or that curriculum will need to be substantially altered if persons who graduate from theological schools are going to be well-equipped to do ministry in the world that awaits them rather than in the world in which their teachers might have been trained!

Training Must Be as Practical as Possible— Mastery of the "classical disciplines" of Bible, theology, and history does not constitute preparation for pastoral ministry. Assuming that pastoral skills can be perfected in field study courses alone (which is how many schools justify their lack of attention to what they call practical ministry) or that such skills can be picked up once a person begins serving a local church is shortsighted on the one hand and woefully inadequate on the other hand. Any theological course of study that requires a massive dose of biblical language study but defines as electives courses in preaching, pastoral care, church polity, group dynamics, church administration, leadership skills, and pastoral self-care techniques may be turning out well-read graduates, but it is not turning out persons who know how to function as pastors upon their graduation.

Medical school and law school graduates are trained to practice their skill sets immediately upon graduation, and that is guaranteed by the need of those graduates to satisfy a bar exam or a medical board certification process. By and large our seminaries do not function this way, and neither do many Christian denominations. Seminaries make sure their graduates can exegete a Hebrew or Greek text, but they are not as committed to being sure their graduates know how to employ that same biblical text in a Sunday morning sermon or midweek Bible class or in the context of a hospital call or a funeral. Students may have studied the doctrine of the incarnation of Jesus Christ, but they may not know a thing about the ministry of presence, which is how the pastor so often extends the presence of Christ to people in times of personal crisis.

Shepherds Also Require Theological Preparation

Do not misunderstand me. In emphasizing the need for practical, on-the-ground ministry training, I am not suggesting that a seminary education and theological preparation are unnecessary or irrelevant. In fact, one of the problems I perceive with ministry in the twenty-first century is that it is being attempted by too many people who are inadequately trained when it comes to vocational skills and biblical and theological knowledge. There is more to being ordained into the Christian ministry than the confidence that "the Lord called me to preach." That call to preach should be followed by a time of structured preparation and training in the relevant fields of Bible, theology, ethics, preaching, counseling, doctrine, church history, and polity. I do not doubt the power of the Holy Spirit to inspire and even equip people to serve in wonderful ways. But even Jesus required the twelve disciples to "follow me" before he sent them into the world to preach the gospel. I clearly remember the day I announced to my mother that I had been called to the ministry. Her immediate response was that she would do everything in her power to assist me in gaining a thorough liberal arts and theological education. She told me, "I do not want to send another ignorant preacher out into an unsuspecting public."

My uncle Elder James B. Alford was pastor of Progressive Church of God in Christ in Maywood, Illinois, for forty-four years. During those years, that denomination did not place much emphasis on formal education, and finishing college or seminary had no bearing on being ordained into their ministry. But my most lasting impression of my uncle was the size and breadth of his personal library and the rigor with which he applied himself to reading and reflection. When I went for an initial visit to the college from which I eventually graduated, he drove my mother and me to the campus. While my mother and I were exploring campus housing and tuition rates, my uncle was going through the religion and theology holdings in the campus library to see if they were up-to-date and sufficiently challenging. He had not spent one day as a college student himself, but he was the essence of lifelong learning. Despite having earned four academic degrees, I do not think I have yet lived up to the scholarly standards set for me by my uncle who never moved beyond a high school diploma so far as formal training is concerned.

Some people are unable to attend seminary before they begin their work in ministry. Many may not be able to achieve any formal degree in theology whatsoever. That is no excuse for "sending another ignorant preacher out into an unsuspecting public." Look at and learn from James B. Alford, who embodied the words of Paul in 2 Timothy 2:15: "Do your best to present yourself to God as one approved, a worker who does not need to be ashamed and who correctly handles the word of truth" (NIV).

Good Shepherds Need Continuing Education

As Paul Nixon's comment clearly implies, what we need to know to be effective in pastoral ministry is always changing. Therefore, pastors need to be involved in some form of continuing education that allows them to maintain their fitness and readiness for ministry as the years go by and the world around them continues to change. If there is a skill or task a pastor has not mastered at the moment when that skill is needed, it may be necessary to refer that matter to someone else who is presently equipped to handle the problem. In the meantime, I continue to be informed by a lesson I learned from Professor Geddes Hanson during my doctor of ministry studies at Princeton Theological Seminary: "Never wait to figure out how to respond to a problem that you know will confront you sooner or later." Our refusal to respond to a ministry need because we do not know what to do should be an increasingly rare occurrence for those who are shepherding the flock of God.

Continuing education for pastors should include some form of ongoing study and reflection with peers and with a teacher or spiritual mentor. Membership in a clergy group that meets on a regular basis for Bible study and for discussion of best practices in ministry as well as ideas for integrating theology with the issues of the day both locally and nationally would be a good way to start. Many seminaries offer formal classes as a way to do continuing education, providing pastors with the opportunity to return to the classroom and the seminary library and to have direct contact with theological professors or notable experts in various areas of ministry, such as preaching, church planting, human sexuality, interreligious dialogue, and more.

Other professions, such as law and medicine, encourage their members to seek continuing education credits as a way to maintain their license to practice in their field. I am not suggesting that same degree of linkage between continuing education and continuing to engage in ministry. However, there is much that pastors need to learn after they have finished their degree program. How has the practice of worship shifted over the years? What percentage of the population in the United States is either unchurched or "never churched"? What new technologies, not available when some pastors were in school, are now available as ways to improve communication in all areas of pastoral life? The world keeps changing, and pastors must keep track of those changes if they want to be effective in doing ministry at a future point in time.

Theory Must Inform Practice

The goal for this discussion about the first concentric circle is to suggest that the many and varied tasks involved in pastoral ministry should be understood and approached in relationship to a philosophy of ministry in which the pastor is perceived as shepherd. That model guides and informs pastors and congregations as they go about the business of properly shepherding the flock of God.

Effective pastoral care is not simply a long to-do list based on any given pastor's likes or dislikes, skills and competencies, or on the context in which that pastor is invited to perform some pastoral task. One who is the shepherd of the flock in the biblical sense of that image will engage in tasks that will feed, nurture, guide, protect, and otherwise benefit the flock of God. The underlying issue before any task is performed is the philosophy of ministry or the overarching vision of the work of the pastor that informs persons in this vocation as they go about deciding how they will approach their daily work. "Why should I as a pastor-shepherd be involved in this particular task?" is as important a question as deciding "How should this task be done?"

The parting words of Paul to the elders of the church in Ephesus are especially insightful at this point: "Keep watch over yourselves and all the flock of which the Holy Spirit has made you overseers. Be shepherds of the church of God, which he bought with his own blood" (Acts 20:28, NIV).

Notes

1. Samuel D. Proctor and Gardner C. Taylor, *We Have This Ministry: The Heart of the Pastor's Vocation* (Valley Forge, PA: Judson Press, 1996).

2. C. Avery Lee and Gardner C. Taylor, *Perfecting the Pastor's Art: Wisdom from Avery Lee and Gardner C. Taylor* (Valley Forge, PA: Judson Press, 2005).

3. Victor D. Lehman, *The Work of the Pastor* (Valley Forge, PA: Judson Press, 2004).

4. Lee and Taylor, 16–17.

5. Lee and Taylor, 19.

6. Cleophus Larue, *The Heart of Black Preaching* (Louisville: Westminster John Knox, 2000), 20–25.

7. Marvin McMickle, *Deacons in Today's Black Baptist Church* (Valley Forge, PA: Judson Press, 2010).

8. Dottie Rambo, "He Looked beyond My Fault," in *African American Heritage Hymnal* (Chicago: GIA Publications, 2001), 249.

9. William B. Oglesby Jr., *Biblical Themes for Pastoral Care* (Nashville: Abingdon, 1980), 14.

10. Gene Bartlett, *The Authentic Pastor* (Valley Forge, PA: Judson Press, 1978), 35–36.

11. Charles Jaeckle and William A. Clebsch, *Pastoral Care in Historical Perspective* (New York: Aronson, 1964), 32–66.

12. Paul Nixon, *Fling Open the Doors: Giving the Church Away to the Community* (Nashville: Abingdon, 2002), 117.

First-Circle Questions for Consideration

1. What does it mean to be a shepherd of the flock of God?

2. How does Jeremiah 3:15, "I will give you shepherds after my own heart, who will lead you with knowledge and understanding" (NIV), inform your philosophy of ministry?

3. Have you ever exercised the ministry of presence? What were the circumstances and what was the outcome?

4. List five pastoral tasks that must be performed by the shepherd of the flock.

5. In what way is one's call to the ministry instrumental in the performance of one's duties?

6. How do you approach the problem of caring for those sheep that you may not like?

7. Have you had to face any challenges brought on by a multicultural or interfaith event?

8. What do you believe constitutes adequate and necessary preparation for pastoral ministry?

9. Do you have a network of other professionals to whom you can refer persons who need specialized skills that you do not possess?

10. Have you pursued any form of continuing education for ministry since you graduated from your last academic program?

The Second Circle—
The Congregation
That Cares

CHAPTER 7

A Congregation That Cares
for One Another

Many of the Jews had come to Martha and Mary
to console them about their brother.
—John 11:19

As the discussion of a second circle of pastoral care begins, it is useful to be reminded that this book is part of a series of books that
seeks to address the same core issues: Does the church have a
future? Do we deserve one?[1] These two questions arise out of data
that suggests that church growth is slowing, church attendance is
declining, and the influence of churches and clergy on matters of
social policy and public discourse is greatly diminished.

Two of the troubling signs of a weakening church are "a narrowing inward focus and the unraveling of spiritual community."[2]
Therefore, in the first volume of this series, Lee Spitzer presents the
idea of the church as the place where "friendship interfaces with the
church's call to be a community of faith-filled disciples seeking to share
the good news of Jesus Christ with their friends, acquaintances, and
others. Friendship, community, discipleship, evangelism, and social
witness all play starring roles in the church's fulfillment of God's
will."[3] This model provides congregations with a way to avoid both
a narrowing inward focus and the unraveling of spiritual community.

Spitzer talks about four friendship circles that move outward from "best friends, to special friends, to social friends, and finally to casual friends."[4] He then explains the friendship circles by saying, "Friendship circles allow us to map the network of relationships that surround us by placing people either closer or farther away from our hearts or souls....Friendships are placed in a given circle based on our personal evaluation of the friendship's intensity."[5] Spitzer proposes that churches can make themselves stronger by becoming a place where genuine friendship at various levels can be created and sustained. "A healthy congregation attracts new members by providing a safe environment for spiritual growth and positive personal relationships."[6] This growth can be sustained when congregations understand that making friends is an important step toward making disciples.

From Friendship Circles to Circles of Care

Our discussion here is framed not by circles of friendship but by circles of care. The two types of circles are by no means synonymous. Circles of friendship measure the degree of intensity between friends, with intimacy decreasing as the circles move outward from best friends to casual friends. Those levels of friendship determine the ease with which a church can attract new members and then get those new members involved and engaged in the ministries of that congregation.

Circles of care illustrate a somewhat different dynamic in relationships. Rather than measuring relational intimacy and intensity, circles of care represent the expanding influence of pastoral care—from a single pastor administering care to a congregation of church members to a community of faithful disciples ministering to one another, to the local body of Christ reaching out to care for the neighborhood outside its church doors. Spitzer's paradigm advocates evangelism, discipleship, and growth through a network of friendships; our goal is to strengthen congregations by nurturing disciples who are themselves pastoral caregivers—to and with the pastor, to and with one another, and to their neighbors in the community. Thus, the three concentric circles of pastoral care illustrate how the love of Jesus Christ is displayed in ways that always move in an outward direction.

In section 2, we explored the first circle of care—the caring pastor who operates within the shepherding motif and displays genuine love and concern for each member of the flock. However, we also established that the pastor cannot and should not attempt to provide all the care that is needed by the flock. That is where the second circle of pastoral care ripples outward, involving a congregation that has been equipped and empowered to share in the work of the ministry with and to one another. In this circle, the congregation is comprised of members who are willing and able to display care and concern for one another in times of need.

How Is the Work of Pastoral Care Accomplished?

First, let's reiterate the point made in the previous section: Pastoral care cannot and should not be done by the pastor alone. The reason isn't merely that in the average congregation of 100 to 150 members there is more pastoral work than any one person can handle no matter how committed he or she may be. Even more significantly perhaps, Ephesians 4:11-13 seems to mandate that church leaders are responsible for making partners of their parishioners. In other words, pastoring is about disciple making. And so pastors are tasked with equipping the saints (i.e., church members and fellow disciples of Jesus) for the work of *shared* ministry.

The second circle of pastoral care offers a powerful and accessible model for accomplishing that goal. By equipping and encouraging the congregation to show care and concern for one another, even and especially when the pastor is not present, the pastor is communicating a profound message: Christianity is not a spectator sport; the congregation is not to observe and be entertained while the pastor and other professional church staff do all the work of Christian ministry. When members of the church learn to demonstrate and deliver care and concern for one another, they are learning to model themselves after the image of Jesus, whose disciples they claim to be. The second circle of care is needed—for the benefit of pastor and congregation alike.

A Circle-One Request and a Circle-Two Response

One of the most dramatic stories in the Bible is the story of the two sisters Mary and Martha in the days before and after the death of their brother Lazarus. This story tends to be told most often from the first-circle of pastoral care perspective, with a focus on the role of Jesus as he was summoned by these two sisters to the bedside of their seriously ill brother. The story reflects the closeness of the friendship between Jesus and this family from the village of Bethany, only a few miles south of Jerusalem. When the two sisters sent for Jesus, they said to him: "Lord, the one you love is sick" (John 11:3, NIV). This call for help was not coming from persons unknown to Jesus, from strangers whose appeal could be based only on compassion and not on years of companionship. The nature of their relationship was reflected in the words used by Martha and Mary: "Lord, the one you love is sick."

This story takes an unusual turn in verse 5: "Now Jesus loved Martha and her sister and Lazarus. So when he heard that Lazarus was sick, he stayed where he was two more days" (John 11:5-6, NIV). By the time Jesus finally arrived in Bethany, Lazarus had already been dead for four days. Typically, teaching and preaching on this story focuses on why Jesus stayed away and why he wept upon finally arriving (when he knew he planned to raise Lazarus again), and on the theological significance of his response to the sisters.

The story itself continues with all eyes fixed on the words and actions of Jesus. The people at the tomb noted Jesus' tears and wondered why he hadn't come sooner. They reeled in shock when the dead man appeared at the grave entrance still wrapped in burial cloths. It was this miraculous resurrection of Lazarus from the dead that was reported to the chief priest and the Sanhedrin in Jerusalem and that set in motion the plot to put Jesus to death. In short, traditionally we read the story of Lazarus and his sisters entirely from a first-circle of pastoral care perspective—with eyes focused on the Good Shepherd.

Not Everybody Was Waiting for Jesus to Arrive

What often goes unnoticed in this passage is the way in which this same story lifts up a powerful example of a second circle of care at work. Consider in this context what the people in the village of Bethany were doing long before Jesus arrived in town. John 11:19 says, "And many of the Jews had come to Martha and Mary to console them about their brother." Not everybody was simply waiting for Jesus to arrive and do his thing.

Without consulting with the local rabbi or being commissioned by Jesus himself, many people took it upon themselves to show up at the home of Mary and Martha to console them over the loss of their brother. Those were the shoulders Mary and Martha had to lean on while Jesus was delayed in his arrival. Those two sisters were not left abandoned in their grief. "Many of the Jews had come to Martha and Mary to console them about their brother." A second circle of care was already at work, even though the initial request from the two sisters was made to Jesus, who represents the first circle of pastoral care in this story.

The text does not go into great detail about what those persons did when they went to that home in Bethany. But to this day, a common custom in the Jewish community when someone dies is for friends and neighbors to show up at the home of the grieving family to "sit shivah." *Shivah* is the Hebrew word for seven, so the phrase "sit shivah" refers to the custom of sitting in grief for seven days after the death and burial of a loved one.

During those seven days, friends and neighbors come to the home of the grieving family and mourn with them. Mary and Martha were sitting shivah after the death of their brother. That fact alone is an indication that any hope of a miracle was already passed. Lazarus was dead, and their neighbors came to comfort and console the sisters concerning their brother.

"Sitting Shivah" Is a Time for Showing Care and Concern— Now as then, visitors to the home of a grieving family bring food so those who are "sitting in their grief" don't have to worry about preparing meals. But the most important thing visitors bring is their physical presence and emotional support. The ministry of presence integral to sitting shivah is a valued and expected part of membership in a faith community. The presence of a rabbi (or pastor) is not essential, although he or she typically pays a visit as well. More significantly, sitting shivah is an instance in which members of the community show love and concern for one another. No profound theological lessons are expected from those who show up. Rather, the gift and the blessing are in the presence, prayers, and practical support of those who come.[7]

Grief Is a Time When a Second Circle Is Needed— The scenario in John 11:19 is a splendid example of the second circle of pastoral care at work. People of faith sprang into action in support of their friends and neighbors, based not merely on personal relationship with the grieving family, but also in response to a clear sense of religious duty and discipline. The actions of the people in ancient Bethany should serve as an example to Christians everywhere nearly two thousand years later. An enormous significance is attached to the idea of people in the faith community reaching out to and caring for one another without requiring the clergy's initiation or presence during such a response.

One of the simplest yet most significant ways by which church members can share in the second circle of care is to be present with one another in times of grief. Death is a regular visitor in all congregations, and there is an expected protocol of response so far as the pastor or other clergy are concerned. In the first circle of care, the pastor is expected to visit the home of the bereaved person or family to begin talking about funeral arrangements and planning the service and interment.

What John 11:19 clearly demonstrates, however, is the role that members of the faith community can perform for one another, tasks that in no way replicate or replace the necessary work going on in the first circle of care. In the next chapter, we will consider some examples of ministry programs that allow congregations to respond in times of loss and grief in practical and caring ways. For now, let it suffice to observe that the Jews in Bethany did not wait until Jesus arrived to attend to Mary and Martha. They were already at the sisters' home offering comfort and consolation when Jesus arrived.

A Phone Call for Help

I came to appreciate the need for a second circle of care very early in my ministry at St. Paul Baptist Church in Montclair, New Jersey. I was called as pastor in September 1976. My official duties began on January 1, 1977. I was scheduled to be installed on the fourth Sunday of February. Then, on the fourth Sunday of January 1977, I received a phone call from a church member. Of course, I did not know this woman very well, having only been at the church for less than a month. However, I *was* her pastor, and she was in need of pastoral care.

This woman told me in that telephone call that her husband of fifty-eight years had just died, and she had just left the nursing home where he had been residing. She wondered if I would come by her home later that evening and sit with her as she worked through the grieving process. Of course, I was willing, but an enormous sense of inadequacy swept over me after I agreed and hung up the phone. After all, at age twenty-eight, I had been married for less than two years. What could I possibly say to comfort a newly bereaved woman who had been married more than twice as long as I had been alive?

I had no deep well of experience in such matters, personally or pastorally. I had taken no course in college or seminary that had prepared me for this encounter. I had given eulogies in the past, but never before had I felt the full weight of being "the pastor" in such a setting.

There was no time to consult my library for any book that might give me a quick primer on "making visits to elderly members of the church who have just lost a longtime spouse during your first year as pastor." It was a Sunday afternoon, and within two hours I would be walking into the home of a woman who needed all the care and comfort that could possibly be provided. She was calling on her pastor within a first-circle of care context. But I knew at once I needed some help and needed it in a hurry.

The Second Circle at Work— In the midst of my anxiety, it occurred to me that one of the women who had served on the pastoral search committee could be invaluable at a moment like this. She had recently lost her husband of many years. She was also a longtime friend of the grieving member who had just called me. While I was more than willing to show up as the representative of the first circle of pastoral care, I knew that this older laywoman would be able to offer a level of care I could not deliver. I called her and explained the circumstances, and she quickly and gladly agreed to accompany me on this pastoral call.

When we arrived at the home, it was obvious that I had made the right decision. The bereaved widow saw who I had brought with me. She locked her eyes on the face of her friend, suddenly realizing that *hers* was really the voice she needed to hear while dealing with the death of her spouse. Recognizing that my presence was not immediately required, I left the two of them alone for a while as one member of that faith community cared for another in a way I never would have been able to do. I later returned to begin talking about funeral arrangements and to end our time together with prayer and Scripture. It was during the first house call, in my first month as solo pastor, that I came to the realization that pastoral care cannot—and should not—be done by the pastor alone. Sometimes the congregation can and should be caring for one another.

A Caring Congregation at Heart

If a caring pastor is the heart of the first circle, then a caring congregation is the heart of the second circle. Again, this concept is based on Ephesians 4:11-13, which calls pastors and church teachers to equip the saints (i.e., church members) to do the work of the ministry. That biblical mandate leads to the model of the three concentric circles of care in which the responsibility and opportunity for displaying the love and concern of Jesus Christ may begin with the pastor, but it does not and should not be limited to one minister.

In the great judgment scene in Matthew 25:31-46, it is not pastors alone who will be held accountable for the service they have given during their lifetime. Clergy and laity alike will have to stand before God and give an account of themselves and their work on behalf of the kingdom. Responding to those who are hungry, thirsty, naked, sick, and imprisoned is pastoral care that occurs when a caring congregation extends its love and concern to one another without having to be prompted by the clergy.

A great benefit of second-circle pastoral care is that more work can be accomplished because more hands are available. More places can be touched because more people are on the move. New leaders and new sets of skills and talents are being developed because more people are working and praying together to address problems and to deliver various forms of care. I have been pleasantly surprised over the years by the number of people willing to move from watching to working when a clear task is set before them, when adequate training has been provided, and when reasonable goals and expectations have been established. It is not just pastors and other clergy who want to answer God with the words of Isaiah 6:8: "Here am I; send me!"

Complacency of a congregation is too often compounded and enabled by clergy who assume that "proper" ministry can be entrusted only to the pastor. So not only do the people need to be trained and equipped, but the pastors need to be reeducated to share in the work of the ministry. As the Good Shepherd to the sheep, Jesus ensured that the sheep learned how to watch out for and care for one another. Today that is how church members become Christian disciples, empowered by the Spirit and entrusted with the gospel ministry of pastoral care within the congregation. I encourage every pastor to create a second circle of pastoral care in the churches where you serve. This is not an attempt to avoid your duties; it is a part of your obligation to inform, equip, and encourage the members of your church to embrace the duties that God expects from each one of them as well.

Notes

1. Lee B. Spitzer, *Making Friends, Making Disciples: Growing Your Church through Authentic Relationships* (Valley Forge, PA: Judson Press, 2010), iv.

2. Spitzer, v.

3. Spitzer, ix.

4. Spitzer, 56.

5. Spitzer, 56.

6. Spitzer, 69.

7. I am indebted to my colleague Rabbi Sharon Stone of Suburban Temple in Beachwood, Ohio, for her help in properly interpreting this Jewish ritual that was recorded in the Gospel of John. I also learned about this contemporary example of sitting Shiva through this article by Joseph Berger, "Sitting Shiva: Trying to Cope with the Loss of a Child," *New York Times*, July 16, 2011, A15.

CHAPTER 8

The Second Circle of Care in Scripture

*Now the whole group of those who believed
were of one heart and soul, and no one claimed private
ownership of any possessions, but everything they
owned was held in common.*
—Acts 4:32

Both the Old and New Testaments offer pastors and congregations examples of second-circle pastoral care in action. In this chapter, we will examine several narratives that demonstrate the need for such care as well as its benefits—to the leader, to the second-circle caregivers, and to the community of faith as a whole. Let us begin with the Hebrew Scriptures and that hero of Judeo-Christian faith, Moses. In his life story, we find two powerful instances where he learned the value of second-circle pastoral care.

Moses as Beneficiary of Second-Circle Care
In Exodus 17:8-13 the people of Israel came under attack by the Amalekites as they made their way from slavery in Egypt to an encounter with God at Mount Sinai. There was no question that Moses was the leader of the Israelites as they faced this threat at a place called Rephidim, but there was more work to be done than Moses could possibly have accomplished by himself.

Someone had to do the fighting and lead the ragtag army. But someone also needed to intercede on behalf of God's people to ensure that God would fight with them. Recognizing that he could not fight the physical and spiritual battle simultaneously, Moses delegated. He instructed Joshua to go with the army and defend the people from the attack by the Amalekites. Meanwhile, while the battling was raging below, Moses went up to the top of a hill to oversee the conflict on a spiritual level. The battle plan was straightforward: as long as the hands of Moses could hold up the staff of God, the Israelites would prevail in the battle. As the battle dragged on, Moses' hands grew weary, and the staff grew heavy, dragging Moses' arm down with its weight. As soon as the staff lowered, the Amalekites seized the advantage in the battle below, but when Moses jerked it back up into place, the tide turned back toward Israel. Clearly Moses had an essential role to play if the nation was to survive, but it was equally clear that he was going to need some help from people within the faith community.

That is when Aaron and Hur entered the story. They did not see this moment as a career opportunity for themselves. They did not attempt to remove the staff from the hands of Moses. Rather, they willingly played a supportive role. First, they found a stone on which Moses could sit while he was holding up the staff. Later they took positions on either side of Moses and held up his hands so that the staff could remain elevated and in clear view. Between the work being done by Joshua in the valley as he battled the Amalekites and the work being done by Aaron and Hur on the hilltop as they supported Moses' hands and arms, Israel was able to gain the victory that day.

Aaron and Hur were members of the second circle of care for Israel in general and for Moses in particular. Their leader, Moses, was present and in the midst of performing a first-circle act of care; he was holding up the staff of God so the army could see it and be empowered. But Moses' arms grew weary, and unless someone had come to help him, the battle would have been lost. Aaron and Hur assisted Moses, offering support that was invaluable if the mission was to be accomplished. Their help was needed at a critical moment, when a leader could not perform an essential role without assistance. The help that Moses needed came from the second circle of care. Bear in mind also that while Aaron and Hur were directing their second circle of care toward Moses, others were offering a similar kind of care on behalf of all the people in that community. Of course, Joshua and the army of Israel were engaged in battle against the Amalekites and others as the people made their way across the Sinai and into Canaan. However, Moses' life offers another example of a second circle of pastoral care that should be highlighted, and we turn to it now.

Another Example of Second-Circle Care for Moses— The story of Moses and his father-in-law, Jethro, in Exodus 18:14-23 offers a wonderful example of the value of the second circle of pastoral care. Jethro chastised his son-in-law for taking on too much work and advised Moses on how to draw others in the faith community into the role of caring for one another. The encounter began with Jethro asking this question of Moses after seeing the younger man working from morning to night with no help: "What is this you are doing for the people? Why do you alone sit as judge, while all these people stand around you from morning till evening?" (v. 14, NIV).

Moses answered Jethro with words that might fall from the lips of any caring pastor who wants to be faithful to the ministry: "Because the people come to me to seek God's will. Whenever they have a dispute, it is brought to me, and I decide between the parties and inform them of God's decrees and instructions" (vv. 15-16, NIV). Jethro responded to Moses with wise words that I now direct to every pastor who is trying to accomplish alone all of the pastoral care needed within the congregation and the community:

What you are doing is not good. You and these people who come to you will only wear yourselves out. The work is too heavy for you; you cannot handle it alone....Select capable men from all the people—men who fear God....Have them serve as judges for the people at all times, but have them bring every difficult case to you; the simple cases they can decide themselves. That will make your load lighter, because they will share it with you. If you do this and God so commands, you will be able to stand the strain, and all these people will go home satisfied. (Exodus 18:17-23)

As pastors, we need to understand the importance and urgency of equipping and encouraging the congregation members to do the work of the ministry, a great portion of which is pastoral care and concern. There are three immediate benefits in equipping the church for service, as seen in Jethro's conversation with Moses:

1. The risk of clergy burnout is reduced.
2. A new set of leaders within the ranks of the church are identified and deployed. This is a kind of disciple making in accordance with Jesus' model as well. As leaders, pastors are wise to cultivate a new generation of leaders who will ensure the future of the ministry as well as its expansion in and beyond the congregation.
3. The needs of the people are addressed with efficiency and effectiveness. More hands result in more work being attempted and hopefully accomplished. More meals can be prepared for grieving families, more flowers can be delivered to shut-in members, more visits can be made to persons in hospitals and nursing homes, and more people can be picked up and driven on church vans when a second circle of care is at work in the church.

Moses Was No Less a Leader for Accepting Assistance— Both of these cases involving Moses revealed a need for support of the primary leader by the efforts of others. Moses was in no way diminished in his authority or leadership because he accepted counsel from Jethro or the help of others who took some of the work off his shoulders and empowered him to accomplish his tasks more effectively. The work of the first circle of care was achieved with the help of those who created a second circle of care around Moses.

Pastors and congregations alike may benefit from observing how the example of Moses in these two stories serves as an approach to ministry they should adopt for themselves. Clergy may appreciate how Moses' willingness to accept help did not diminish or replace his role as leader. Instead, the support of others allowed Moses to function more effectively—for the health of the leader and for improved service to the community of faith. More of the work of the ministry can be accomplished when more people are involved in accomplishing the tasks at hand. Others sharing in the ministry work frees the pastor to devote more time and attention to those cases or tasks in which she or he must operate alone. The church as a whole is better served when the person at the center of the first circle of pastoral care is supported by persons who create a second circle of care.

New Testament Examples of Second-Circle Care

With such notable examples in the Hebrew Scriptures, it shouldn't be surprising to find that Jesus and the first-century church also bore witness to the power and potential of pastoral care in the second circle. Let us begin with a story from the Gospels and then look at the book of Acts.

Help for One Who Needed to Be Healed— Mark 2:1-5 provides another example of how the second circle of care may be enacted. It involves a man who was paralyzed being carried to Jesus by four unnamed men who hoped that Jesus would heal their friend.

The background for this story actually starts with Mark 1:32 where people in and around Capernaum began to bring sick people to Jesus to be healed by him as he had done both for the mother-in-law of Simon and for a man who was cleansed of an unclean spirit. Verses 32-34 say: "That evening after sunset the people brought to Jesus all the sick and demon-possessed. The whole town gathered at the door, and Jesus healed many who had various diseases. He also drove out many demons." The practice of bringing the sick to Jesus is continued in Mark 2:1-5 when he returned to Capernaum, the scene of his first miraculous healings. When people came to Jesus on their own power, as the leper did by calling loudly to Jesus as he passed by in Mark 1:40-45, their encounter with Jesus was a first-circle event. However, for those who required the assistance of strangers or friends to bring them to Jesus' attention, that encounter is the direct result of the second circle of care. While being healed by Jesus was still the ultimate objective, what was first required were some helping hands from within a caring community.

The Faith of Four Restored the Body of One— The story of the healing of the paralyzed man in Mark 2 is a wonderful illustration of the second circle in action. In order for him to be healed, he needed the help of four men who would literally carry him into Jesus' presence. Four nameless men formed a second circle of care for the paralytic. The first circle of care (Jesus) was sitting just inside a house not many feet away. The healing the paralyzed man needed was well within reach, but he could not access the healing because he could not bring himself into Jesus' presence.

John 5:1-8 records the story of another man whose paralysis made him dependent on the assistance of others for his healing. The man had sat by the pool of Bethesda for thirty-eight years waiting to be healed when an angel of the Lord periodically troubled the waters of that pool. He had been waiting for almost four decades for a second circle of care to intervene on his behalf. After such a long wait, he finally encountered Jesus and received his healing via the first circle of care. But how tragic that he had to wait thirty-eight years when wholeness was at hand, if only the community of faith had intervened with an act of pastoral care!

In Mark 2 the story develops differently. Jesus was inside a house healing and teaching those who were inside with him. The paralyzed man in this instance was probably as close to Jesus as the man in John 5 was to the waters of the Pool of Bethesda. Who knows how long that man would have remained outside of that house and out of reach of his healing if it had not been for four unnamed men? The text does not suggest that Jesus sent those men on a mission of mercy, nor does it suggest that the paralyzed man had solicited their help. Apparently, four people came together on their own initiative to form a circle of care for a paralytic. They picked him up while he lay on his pallet, and they brought him to the house where Jesus was sitting.

Caring for Others Often Requires Extra Effort— Of course, this story not only celebrates the second circle of care demonstrated by those four men; it also points out how far they were willing to go to accomplish what they had set out to do. The men were attempting to bring the paralyzed man into Jesus' presence in hopes that the man could be healed. When they arrived at the house where Jesus was seated, they discovered that the building was crammed with people to the point that the doors could not open or close. Every available inch of space was filled with others who had arrived ahead of them. The men could have shrugged to themselves and said to the paralyzed man, "Well, we tried!" They could have looked at the scene before them and concluded that their efforts, while well-intentioned, were apparently all in vain. There was no more room in the house for another person in need.

Much to the surprise of everyone in that house, these men came up with a resourceful solution. Rather than turning away in resignation, they decided to lift the paralyzed man up onto the roof of the house. Then they opened a hole in the roof and began to lower the paralyzed man down into Jesus' presence while that man was still lying on his pallet. The owner of that house might well have been shocked and outraged to have someone destroy his roof like that! However, Jesus had an altogether different response as he saw these four men straining to lower a paralyzed man into his presence. Mark 2:5 says, "When Jesus saw their faith, he said to the paralytic, 'Son, your sins are forgiven.'" The paralyzed man was healed by his friends' faith!

"Their Faith" Was the Second Circle of Care— What is most notable in this passage about the four men is how it highlights how others in the community assume responsibility in caring for one another. "Their faith" was on display on behalf of someone other than themselves. "Their faith" got the paralyzed man to the door of the house where Jesus was seated. "Their faith" caused the man to be lifted up onto the roof and then lowered down into Jesus' presence. "Their faith" moved Jesus into action.

These four men are a reminder that there are times in the life of the faith community when it is *our faith* that must be on display. *Our faith* must be at work on behalf of someone in need. *Their faith* may have taken them as far as they can go. What is needed when *their faith* has reached its limit is for *our faith* to reach in and come to their aid. This passage in Mark 2 is a wonderful example of what a second circle of pastoral care can accomplish when persons who are moved by their own faith in God are willing to come to the aid of others in a time of need. There is no indication that Jesus sent those men outside to bring the paralyzed man into his presence. There is no suggestion that the local rabbi sought them out for this assignment. There is no reason to believe that any of those men shared some close family relationship with the paralyzed man. The only thing that can be concluded is that these men took it upon themselves to attend to the man's needs. They did not have the power themselves to heal that man, to restore strength to his legs and the power to walk, but they knew somebody who could do exactly that. Here is a compelling case of people caring for one another within the community of faith.

Care without Recognition— There was no interest in who would get the credit for this act of love and kindness. No one sought out the four men after the fact for special recognition. As with Aaron and Hur, no testimonial dinner was held in their honor to reward them for their service. But unlike Aaron and Hur, who are known for assisting Moses, nothing is known about the four men who came to the aid of the paralytic in Mark 2. No names are given and no information provided about their status in the community or even about their previous relationship with the paralyzed man. All we know is that "some men came, bringing to [Jesus] a paralyzed man" (v. 3, NIV).

As the Bible recounts their story, it is not their identity or their names that are significant. What is important is what they did. Pastors should equip the people in their churches to focus on this example of people caring for one another even to the point of extra effort and exertion. Every local church becomes a better and stronger community when the members are willing to demonstrate care and concern for one another with no regard for recognition, reward, or repayment. When that happens, those persons are prepared to do the work of the ministry whether the pastor is present or not.

The Second Circle Helps Guard against an Overworked Pastor— Do you recall the three lessons from the story of Jethro advising Moses? It isn't only God's people who benefit from pastoral care in the second circle. The leader, the pastor, is also a beneficiary when second-circle care is truly in the hands of the church members.

At various times, concerned church members attempt to add something new to the pastor's already crowded plate of responsibilities. "We need a ministry to members who are divorced, who are depressed, and who are bereaved," these concerned members might say in concern. "Pastor, why don't you form support groups for them? And what about establishing a transportation ministry to help get seniors and handicapped members to and from church activities and midweek appointments?" It may never occur to these concerned persons that they could undertake some of these ministries on their own without drawing the pastor into more work.

An all-too-common "let the pastor do it" mentality exists in far too many churches today. When that mind-set governs, it usually indicates that people are stuck with a traditional sense of pastoral care in which clergy are expected to do all the work of ministry. Indeed, even some pastors feel guilty if they do not accept every assignment offered to them from within the ranks of the congregation. The circles of care model challenges pastors and congregations alike to resist this pastor-centric ministry mind-set. Such a view of ministry creates a fellowship of passive and underutilized members and produces a pastor who is burned out and overworked.

Notice in contrast that Jesus didn't intervene when the hole in the roof opened. He didn't say, "There's no need for you to destroy property—I'll come outside to you!" or "I see your faith from here and I'll heal him from here before you risk injuring your backs!" Jesus waited and watched while four humble men from the community of faith cared for someone in need.

What if pastors began to respond to concerned members with an invitation to step in and assume some personal responsibility for the very need they have identified? What if the pastor said, "What would you like to do to respond to that concern?" instead of wearily making a note and promising, "I'll look into that this week"? Some members will eagerly embrace being actively involved in doing the work of the ministry; others will need to be educated and encouraged in doing so. The pastor may need to take the first step in initiating a process by which a second circle of care is created. But once it is underway, there will be a great many areas of ministry in which members of the church can be engaged without adding to the pastor's workload.

The Second Circle of Care in the Early Church— The idea of putting an underutilized faith community to work is perfectly modeled by Peter in Acts 6:1-6. In my book *Deacons in Today's Black Baptist Church*,[1] I make the point that Peter was determined not to assume more responsibilities than he and the other apostles could manage alone. He had been made aware of an act of discrimination within the early Christian community in which the widows of Greek Christians were receiving far less from the commonly held pool of funds than the widows of Palestinian Christians. The text makes it clear that those who raised this issue with Peter were fully expecting him and the other apostles to step in and resolve this problem. The community saw this as a first-circle of pastoral care issue.

Peter saw things differently and moved immediately toward the formation of a second circle of care to which this responsibility could be assigned. The issue that was being raised was important and the act of racial or ethnic discrimination was real. But in Peter's mind, the existence of a problem did not necessarily mean that the apostles were the ones who had to step in and solve it. Peter seemed determined that he was not going to expand his workload to take upon himself the added responsibility for a task that he believed others in the community could perform just as well as he or the apostles. That decision by Peter is what gave birth to the office of the *diakonoi*, or deacons.

The need for care to be given to the widows was obvious to Peter and the other apostles, yet they could not attend to the matter without taking away from the time they needed for the ministry of preaching and prayer. Someone else would need to oversee a fairer and more just distribution system for the commonly held goods of the Christian community in Jerusalem.

Peter reached a solution that every pastor needs to replicate when work needs to be done within the church in support of the needs of the membership: "It would not be right for us to neglect the ministry of the word of God in order to wait on tables [care for the basic needs of the people]. Brothers and sisters, choose seven men from among you who are known to be full of the Spirit and wisdom. We will turn this responsibility over to them and will give our attention to prayer and the ministry of the word" (Acts 6:2-4, NIV).

Peter did not doubt that there was work that needed to be done that could rightfully fall under the umbrella of pastoral care. The needs and rights of the Greek widows needed to be addressed and upheld. What Peter also understood was that there were others within the community who could shoulder that burden, take some of the pressure off of him and the other disciples, and still guarantee that the work was efficiently and effectively done.

Good Things Happen When People Are Empowered— Peter's response to the need for a new ministry was not only to appoint persons from within the Jerusalem church to take charge of that ministry, but to specifically find people that fit the profile he set forth. "Choose seven men from among you who are known to be full of the Spirit and wisdom. We will turn this responsibility over to them" (Acts 6:3, NIV). While Peter and the other apostles would be the ones who would officially commission the work that needed to be done, it was the community itself that would select from among themselves those who would perform the task.

What is interesting to note, then, is that the people in the Jerusalem church picked seven individuals, each of whom has a Greek name: Stephen, Philip, Procorus, Nicanor, Timon, Parmenas, and Nicolas from Antioch. In an attempt to address a problem of racial discrimination against the Greek-speaking widows, the church in Jerusalem assigned Greek-speaking deacons not only to advocate for those widows, but to oversee the entire benevolent operation of the church. What a comfort it must have been to the Greek-speaking widows and what a time of encouragement it must have been for the other Greek-speaking members of that early church community when persons from their ethnolinguistic heritage were elevated to leadership positions.

That was no small matter in first-century Jerusalem, which was still home to the idea that all Greek converts to the faith were to be numbered among the despised Gentiles unless and until they first adhered to certain Jewish laws such as circumcision and dietary codes. Much of Paul's ministry was devoted to resolving this schism within the early church, and the first major council of the church convened to address the place of Gentile converts to Christianity (see Acts 15).

But while the leaders of the church were busy debating the increasing diversity of their community, the members of the Jerusalem church had already indicated their views. With this one single act described in Acts 6:3, the members of the church seemed ready and willing to embrace Greek converts as brothers and sisters. (It is also interesting to note that this form of racial discrimination within the Jerusalem church is never mentioned again.) A second-circle of care ministry was set in place, and a serious problem was resolved once and for all.

Leaders in the Second Circle Should Be Spiritually Mature— The story about the formation of a second circle of care in Acts 6 provides an opportunity to talk some more about leadership development in the local church. Peter did not instruct the Jerusalem church to go out and choose the first seven people they came across and make them responsible for this sensitive second-circle ministry. Instead, he set forth a short list of spiritual qualities that we in the twenty-first-century church would do well to consider when calling on lay members to aid the pastor in doing certain ministry work.

Different versions of the Bible use different words for the attributes listed in Acts 6:3. The New International Version says that Peter instructed the church to look for "men who are known to be full of the Spirit and wisdom." The New Revised Standard Version offers a slightly different rendering: "men of good standing, full of the Spirit and of wisdom." The American Standard Version says, "men of good report, full of the Spirit and of wisdom," and the English Standard Version says, "men of good repute, full of the Spirit and of wisdom." The actual Greek word translated "standing," "report," and "repute" is *marturoumenous*, which has as one of its usages in the New Testament the idea of receiving a good report from those who speak about someone else. The word is most famously used in Acts 1:8 when Jesus tells his disciples, "You will be my witnesses in Jerusalem, in all Judea and Samaria, and to the ends of the earth." In Acts 6:3, the challenge is not to the church to be a witness about the mission and ministry of Jesus, but to the Jerusalem church to select leaders about whom everyone who knows them has a good report. They did not have to be perfect people, but they were to be above reproach in their public lives. Why entrust a major ministry responsibility to people who were already being talked about openly for being dishonest, unreliable, uncooperative, and/or more interested in giving orders to others than in offering service to those in need?

Being in Good Standing Is Not about Membership— Church members who are involved in the second circle of care should also be "persons in good standing." In many churches the term "good standing" means only that such persons have made some financial contribution to the church in the previous calendar year; it may not even entail contributions equal to the traditional tithe (10 percent of one's income). Financial standing may speak to the issue of membership in a local church, but it does not necessarily resolve the larger and more important issue of discipleship as a follower of Jesus Christ. The kind of work involved in the second circle should not be assigned to persons whose only attribute is that they "paid their dues" to the church.

What Peter had in mind is the selection of people who are known to be regular in their church attendance, known to be prayerful and reverent, and known to be honest and trustworthy in word and deed. Churches make a grave mistake when they assign people to important ministry areas based primarily on attributes that earn respect in the corporate or academic worlds but that have nothing to do with Christian maturity. A good public school teacher is not necessarily the wisest choice to serve as superintendent of the church's Sunday school program. The church needs to determine if that teacher is in good standing as far as spiritual formation is concerned. In addition to knowledge about curriculum development and pedagogy, that teacher must also possess other attributes that reflect a life lived in obedience to the teachings of Christ.

A corporate executive would not necessarily make for a great church trustee, unless that person also possessed some of the spiritual gifts of 1 Corinthians 12:7-10 or some of the fruit of the Spirit as set forth in Galatians 5:22-23. I have seen something happen in churches over and over again involving the corporate mentality as the model for how to organize and operate a church. Faith is sacrificed for efficiencies. Compassion for the poor and needy is replaced by "fiduciary responsibilities." Maintaining the church's finances often leads to a power struggle in which trustees want to regulate every aspect of church life and rule over the church staff and volunteers—including the pastor! These persons do not attend

Bible study or prayer meetings. They do not contribute much to the discussion about how to better serve the needs of the poor. In some cases, they collect the Sunday morning offering and leave the sanctuary to count the money while the worship service, including the sermon, goes on in their absence.

If a church is to have an effective second-circle ministry, then lay leaders need to be in good standing; they need to be spiritually mature and Christlike in word and deed. To be sure, everyone can volunteer for *some* aspect of the work of the ministry. A willing heart and a helping hand are always needed. But those who agree to serve within the ranks of the second circle of care should have a heart that has been shaped by the teachings of the gospel and a hand that is extended to give and serve without seeking any reward or benefit in return. Pastors must follow the example of Peter and be sure that some criteria exist by which spiritual standards and expectations for lay leadership are determined. The first step is to look for people who enjoy a good reputation and good standing within the congregation.

Full of the Spirit and of Wisdom— As a way of spelling out what good reputation might entail, Peter urged the church to find persons full of the Spirit and of wisdom. The church was to look for persons who displayed what might best be referred to as godliness. These are people who exhibit a level of spirituality and insight that goes beyond mere church attendance. In 2 Peter 1:5-9, Peter expands on what being full of the Spirit and of wisdom looks like: "For this very reason, make every effort to add to your faith goodness; and to goodness, knowledge; and to knowledge, self control; and to self-control, perseverance; and to perseverance, godliness; and to godliness, mutual affection; and to mutual affection, love. For if you possess these qualities in increasing measure, they will keep you from being ineffective and unproductive in your knowledge of our Lord Jesus Christ" (NIV).

Too many members of local churches are just that: ineffective and unproductive in their knowledge of Jesus Christ. Part of the work of the pastor is to equip such people to engage in the work of the ministry. These are among the things that are involved in "equipping the church." When these persons have been properly equipped, they will be more likely to share within the second circle of pastoral care in their local church, and their service will likely be directed more to the glory of God than to the gratification of their own ego.

If I Can Help Somebody as I Pass Along

The objective of choosing women and men who are full of the Spirit and of wisdom, who will assume responsibility and take leadership in the second circle of pastoral care, is to increase the likelihood that every local church will be shaped and molded in such a way that they will eagerly embrace the words of the song made famous by Mahalia Jackson that says:

> If I can help somebody as I pass along;
> If I can cheer somebody with a word or song;
> If I can show somebody that they're travelling wrong,
> Then my living will not be in vain.

> If I can do my duty as a Christian ought;
> If I can bring back beauty to a world gone wrought;
> If I can spread love's message like the master taught,
> Then my living will not be in vain.[2]

Notes

1. Marvin A. McMickle, *Deacons in Today's Black Baptist Church* (Valley Forge, PA: Judson Press, 2010).

2. Alma Bazel Androzzo, "If I Can Help Somebody," © copyright 1944 by Laflour Music Ltd.

CHAPTER 9

Practical Examples of Second-Circle Ministry

Those who say, "I love God," and hate their brothers or sisters,
are liars; for those who do not love a brother or sister whom
they have seen, cannot love God whom they have not seen.
—1 John 4:20, NRSV

In chapter 8 we considered a series of biblical examples from the Old and New Testaments to make the point that caring for one another has deep roots within the Judeo-Christian tradition. In this chapter, we will explore some practical ministries that can be established by local churches as they seek to establish and sustain a second circle of pastoral care. Not every local church can or should maintain all of the second-circle ministries listed here. Indeed, each congregation will want to discern among its leadership and members what needs are most critical and what ministries are best suited to meet those needs. Moreover, not every church may choose to address the problems in the same way. My intention is not to dictate the form in which ministries are provided. That should be done by the individual local church body with an awareness of that church's structure and resources. Nevertheless, I do want to highlight certain functions that local churches may want to replicate in whatever ways seem most suitable for them as they attempt to be a caring people. My intention in this chapter is merely to offer ideas and examples of what a local church can do as members seek to provide care and support for one another.

How Wide Is Our Second Circle of Care?

Before I begin to talk about the functions of persons caring for one another, we must consider a separate question: How wide will we allow our circle of care to become? In other words, whose burdens of sin or sorrow will we be willing to bear? Whose sickness will touch our hearts and prod us into action? For whom will we be willing to pray? Local churches should seek to do everything listed in this chapter and more, allowing for variations based on locale, social context, and economic resources.

The question, therefore, is not *whether* a local church should offer ministries of care and concern as an extension of the work of ministry. It is *who will be included or excluded*, for any reason, from the second circle of care of any given local church. Which members of the church might be overlooked or ignored, left outside the circle of love and care? Every contemporary Christian church needs to be careful that it is not behaving like the church in Jerusalem in Acts 6 that neglected the widows of Greek-speaking members of their congregation.

An American Express Card slogan proclaims, "Membership has its privileges." That means that anyone issued an American Express Card is entitled to certain services and conveniences not available to noncardholders. Does that same principle apply in our churches? Does every local church member have privileges when it comes to being cared for, prayed for, visited, remembered, included, and supported in times of need?

When Did We See You Hungry?— In Matthew 25:31-46, Jesus set forth actions of compassion and concern that are the marks of his disciples. Jesus said, "I was hungry, thirsty, naked, sick, a stranger, in prison." Those to whom he was speaking in that passage said in response, "When did we see you in any of those conditions?" The point was one of two possible responses. First, if they had known it was Jesus who was in need of their assistance, they surely would have responded. Second, they did not respond because the person in need was not Jesus or anyone else of real importance in their lives. Jesus used that eschatological image to tell us about who should be included in our second circle of care. "Whatever you did for one of the least of these brothers and sisters of mine, you did for me" (Matthew 25:40, NIV). That is the example we should be following.

Of more importance at this point is the dire warning of Jesus in Matthew 25:45: "Whatever you did not do for one of the least of these, you did not do for me" (NIV). If the person in need had been a more prominent member of the congregation, perhaps we would have responded. If he or she had been a deacon or a soloist in the choir, we would have taken action. If this person had been a member of one of the "leading families" in the church, we would have lined up and taken turns to be helpful. But the sad fact is that there are members of all churches who are ignored, overlooked, and neglected, like the Greek-speaking widows in Acts 6, precisely because they are not prominent or popular or pedigreed, and because they are the victims of prejudice of one kind or another.

Whom Are We Excluding?— Diversity within the congregation comes with its own set of challenges. I can remember the days of the "church-growth movement" in the 1980s when the idea of homogeneity was popular. The term *homogeneity* was used to suggest that people did not want to cross many lines of difference— racial, economic, theological, or political—in their search for a church home. In other words, the church-growth advocates said, people want to join churches in which the present membership is as much like them as possible.

The implications of that principle, if still true, are enormous in twenty-first-century America where racial interaction is becoming increasingly common in the workplace, on the social scene, and even in marriage and parenting, but far less often in most churches. Are our churches open to racial and ethnic diversity, or will we be stuck in the nineteenth century with its sharp lines of division, distinction, and discrimination based on race and ethnicity? In Galatians 3:28, Paul says, "There is neither Jew nor Gentile, neither slave nor free, nor is there male and female, for you are all one in Christ Jesus" (NIV). That may be true "in Christ," but is it actually true in most Christian churches?

The truth is, some congregations do not want anyone to join them who is not as much like the existing members as possible. I have seen congregations, especially in racially shifting communities, wither and die simply because the existing members of the church were not open to the new residents who were moving into the community and in search of a new church home. What a shame it is to say that the words of Liston Pope from 1961 are just as true fifty years later: "11:00 Sunday morning is the most racially segregated hour in America."[1]

I have already made the case for why the local church should be equipped to do the work of the ministry, and that ministry has been defined as a second circle of pastoral care. The question now is who are the people in our churches who will or will not be included in a display of care and concern? Will the church care for young girls if they become pregnant out of wedlock? Will the church care for members who contract HIV/AIDS by no matter what method of transmission? Will the church care for members as they age and grow old and can no longer serve or support the church financially as they once did? Is the church a welcoming and supportive environment for ex-offenders who have returned from incarceration and are hoping to be reintegrated into society? Even if a church has not become an affirming community as far as gays and lesbians are concerned, is it at least willing to be a welcoming community where blatant prejudice is not shown and where cruel and hurtful comments are not intentionally hurled whether in sermons or among the members? The sign of a strong second circle in the church is not measured by how the congregation responds when its most prominent and most prosperous members are in need. The eyes of the Lord are always fixed on "the least of these," and the eyes of every local church ought to be willing to extend that far as well.

In What Ways Can We Care for One Another?

Members of a local church should support one another during times of bereavement. A program should be in place to assist persons with transportation needs to and from medical appointments and the grocery store, as well as back and forth to church events. And plans should be made for aiding persons who face short-term financial needs for utility bills, prescription medication, and emergency food relief, as well as for responding to needs following cataclysmic events like fires or floods.

The Helping Hands Club— Having discussed the importance of being willing to care for one another without prejudice or favoritism, let us turn now to the various forms by which such care can be expressed and delivered. As I said earlier, no one form of care delivery is right for every church. For instance, in my first pastoral assignment at St. Paul Baptist Church in Montclair, New Jersey, there was an organization of church members called the Helping Hands Club. They were a warm and wonderful group of older women who made it their ministry to plan, prepare, and serve a meal following the funeral and burial of any church member or family member of a church member. It was amazing to see the smiles on the faces of people returning from the cemetery after burying a loved one as they were greeted at the dinner with love, warm smiles, and big hugs from caring members of their congregation.

This ministry was provided for the family at no cost. Instead, the church budget included a line item to provide funds to purchase food, kitchen supplies, paper goods, and utensils for funeral repasts. Those who served the meal expected nothing in return for their service. They simply wanted to extend a ministry of care and support to a grieving family. From all observations, the members of the Helping Hands Club received as much joy and satisfaction in being together during those times as the families they served received from their kindness and hospitality.

I did not organize the Helping Hands Club upon my arrival at that church; they were already organized. I never had to call them up and remind them to prepare a funeral dinner; they always took the initiative following any death announcement in the congregation to contact the church office and then the bereaved family to extend their services. They were a perfect example of what churches can do as part of creating a second circle of care in which members are equipped and encouraged to show care and concern for one another. The cost is minimal and the staffing is entirely voluntary, but the sense of support and love communicated by this simple ministry is inestimable.

The Hospitality Committee— Much to my surprise and delight, a similar ministry was already in operation when I arrived at my second pastoral assignment at Antioch Baptist Church of Cleveland, Ohio. This group goes by the name of hospitality committee, but the idea is essentially the same. Two teams of people alternate months of serving in this ministry. The total number of volunteers is between ten and twelve, with a team captain for each group. The captain is contacted by the church office when a funeral is being scheduled. The captain then contacts the team members and also contacts the family of the deceased to discuss how many persons will need to be served.

The hospitality committee makes it clear that this is a ministry primarily for the family of the deceased and for any out-of-town visitors. That being said, there always seems to be enough food to serve other members of the congregation who attend the funeral and make the trip from the church to the cemetery and back. The fellowship experienced during those dinners can go on well past the time it takes to eat the meal. Family members have time to spend together before they start heading to their homes both in town and places far away.

The one administrative and budget-related issue that served us well in both congregations was that the church budget covered the food and supply expenses; the labor was provided by volunteer members of the ministry. If a church decides to offer such a ministry, they need to think about how they will budget for these expenses. Some churches may operate out of a unified budget as mentioned here, in which food costs for funerals are a line item in the annual church budget and therefore provided by weekly tithes and offerings. However, some churches may seek to have those expenses covered by a benevolence budget administered by the board of deacons or out of their church office. Again, the issue of form should not obscure the broader issue of function.

The Fellowship Fund— This fellowship fund is a benevolence fund overseen by the board of deacons to which members can turn when they face a modest financial crisis they cannot meet on their own. The needs that have been brought to the fellowship fund have ranged from rent assistance to help with utility bills, prescription drug costs, and groceries. In the church where I serve, no money is ever given to persons who apply to the fellowship fund. Instead, members of the deacon board take the bills in question, and if the request is approved, the bill is paid. If the need for food is real, based on a face-to-face interview, then an agreed-upon shopping list is filled by the deacons and the food is brought to the church where it can be picked up by the needy person or family. Other churches may choose to offer direct financial grants to needy families and individuals, thus leaving those persons to responsibly follow through in resolving the problem or meeting the need.

There are two administrative keys to the operation of this kind of second-circle ministry: funding and verification of the need. In one case, something like our fellowship fund is itself funded by the weekly offerings. An annual amount for this fund is agreed on by the church at the annual meeting, and the funds are accounted for on a quarterly basis. In recent years, that amount has steadily increased as the nation's economic conditions have worsened. Here again, the whole congregation supports this second circle of care through their tithes and offerings. However, the actual hands-on work is done by a small group of persons (the deacons) who consider each request and determine how and when to respond. In another case, churches may raise the funds needed for this ministry through a separate, dedicated offering. Such a special offering could be taken up by the congregation on some regularly scheduled occasion, such as a monthly Communion service. Other occasions can be identified during which these funds can be gathered if a church prefers not to make this area of ministry a line item in its annual budget.

In the manner of Acts 6:1-6, this ministry has been given to our deacons (*diakonoi*). Four or five deacons meet with persons requesting assistance in a confidential setting. They sometimes take advantage of the expertise of other members of the church who work in the social service arena to help them in their deliberations. The names of those who request help are never shared with the entire deacon board, much less with the entire congregation. In my twenty-four years at Antioch, I have referred many people to the fellowship fund, but in most instances even I do not know what the outcome was for a certain case. This is a second-circle ministry in which members of the congregation are demonstrating care and concern for one another. Each request for assistance is responded to with a face-to-face meeting where proof of the need is demonstrated. Matthew 25:31-46 is the operable biblical challenge: "I was hungry, thirsty, naked, sick...," and you gave me some help.

Chariots of Love— One of the great challenges for older people in the congregation is securing transportation to and from various appointments and other locations. Getting to medical or dental appointments on time can be challenging enough when you have your own car and are able to drive yourself around. That problem is compounded when the person who needs to be transported is physically challenged, unable to drive, and too old or sick to take public transportation. What they need more than anything else is a ride to and from their destination. That is where the Chariots of Love come into play.

Chariots of Love is a transportation ministry in which members of the church who own a car make themselves available on a prescheduled basis to transport other members of the congregation to various locations. Imagine being a person with a serious arthritic condition who needs to get to the grocery store but cannot drive and cannot manage getting on and off a public bus. What a blessing it is when someone from the church pulls into the driveway of their home and chauffeurs them around at no cost.

The ministry is advertised in the weekly Sunday bulletin with information about who can be called to coordinate this ministry area. The coordinator arranges the matches between the driver and the person in need of transportation. More often than not the trip ends up involving more than a ride to and from an appointment. The two people involved almost always stop for lunch and a time of fellowship. This ministry tends to be operated by retired members of the congregation who are available during the day when most medical, business, or other personal appointments are scheduled. However, it also operates on the weekend when others in the congregation can get involved.

Seasonal Flowers— Many churches are beautifully decorated for the Christmas and Easter seasons. For four weeks from Advent through Christmas Sunday poinsettias are placed on the window sills of the sanctuary and along the perimeter of the pulpit area. Their beautiful colors add to the worship experience for those who enter the sanctuary each week. On Easter Sunday the sight and scent of lilies fills the sanctuary with their beauty and bouquet.

Most churches have homebound or hospitalized members who are unable to enter the sanctuary at all due to acute illness or prolonged incapacitation. It is almost as if the holiday seasons pass them by while others in the congregation share in the seasonal festivities together. So imagine the joy when there is a knock at the door and members of the congregation show up with a seasonal flower to be displayed in the home or at the hospital bedside of a shut-in. The flower may be accompanied with copies of the weekly church bulletin or newsletter. Churches that have the capability may include a CD or a DVD of a recent worship service or special holiday event that occurred at the church. This ministry extends the care and concern of the congregation beyond the limit of those who are able to be present in the church building.

As with other second-circle of care ministries mentioned above, the cost of the seasonal flowers is figured into the annual budget. A committee uses the church's sick and shut-in list to determine how many flowers are needed. A seasonal flower is provided for every name on that list. The names and addresses are placed on each plant. Then church members are invited to come to where the flowers have been placed and select the person to whom they would like to make a delivery. This takes only minutes to resolve, because most people take a flower to someone who lives or is hospitalized near them and deliver the flower on the way home from church.

Seasonal flowers could also be delivered by members of a Sunday school class, a birth month club, a missionary group, or some other arrangement that may work in that church. There are a variety of ways to fund the cost of the flowers, from the annual budget to individual donations or a corporate sponsor. These costs also might be covered by dedicated offerings taken up during the appropriate holiday season (Advent-Christmas or Lent-Easter).

However the costs are handled, the message of love and remembrance that is communicated by those deliveries is beyond price. One of the painful side effects of being hospitalized or incapacitated for a long period of time is a sense of isolation. It begins to appear that life is passing you by and the world is carrying on without you. That sense of isolation is shattered when a church member walks in the door of your home or hospital room with a seasonal flower that bears your name. That experience can help to make for a merry Christmas or happy Easter.

Lay Shepherds— The shepherding motif coined by Seward Hiltner[2] and referenced repeatedly as an operational model for the work of the pastor in the first circle of care can be helpfully extended to the role of deacons or other lay leaders in a local church. Just as Jethro told Moses that he needed to break the nation of Israel up into thousands and hundreds and tens for easier management, so should the church be broken up into small groups that can be overseen by a deacon or some other designated person. In our church, twenty-five persons are assigned to every deacon, and that deacon (called a shepherd deacon) has the responsibility of keeping up with those twenty-five people throughout the year. The shepherd deacon visits them when they are sick or hospitalized, and is present in the home and in the church when the individual or a member of that person's family has died.

At our church, the primary role of lay shepherding is done by deacons. At each monthly deacons' meeting, the deacons are called on to give an update on anything happening with any of their sheep. Once a year each deacon is encouraged to host a social gathering for his or her sheep. That becomes an occasion when that small group can fellowship together away from the church building. In a large congregation, the existence of small groups that allow for members to really get to know and support each other is invaluable. The program works best when the members of the church do not call the pastor of the congregation as a first response when they have a problem; their first call should be to their shepherding deacon. This is a second-circle ministry in which members are caring for one another without the pastor being involved in any way.

Some churches may choose to approach this issue in another way, particularly in congregations or denominations that do not include a ministry body such as the board of deacons. There is always the possibility that members can care for one another without having any official title attached to them. Some churches have a slogan on their outdoor bulletin board as well as in their weekly church bulletin that says, "Pastor: Rev. John Smith; Ministers: All members." What is being communicated is that some tasks do belong to the professional clergy in every church. At the same time, every member of the congregation can and should feel encouraged to share in the work of the ministry by any means deemed useful by their congregation.

Worldwide Communion— In most Christian churches, the observance of Holy Communion, the Eucharist, or the Lord's Supper— whatever term is used—is a highly anticipated sacred occasion. For those who have been recently baptized or confirmed in the faith, the service takes on even more meaning as they engage in their "first communion." Whether this is done daily, weekly, monthly, or on an even less frequent basis, people look forward to that special service. The forms by which Communion is observed may vary widely from place to place, but the sense of intimacy with God and with other worshippers is the same no matter where the service is held.

What happens to members of the congregation who are unable to be present at the Communion service due to sickness, employment, family responsibilities, or inclement weather? It is a wonderful thing if their local church is organized in such a way that on a scheduled basis Communion is carried to those church members who cannot get out to the church to share in that observance with the other members of the congregation. The easiest way to do this is to use a set rotation every year that can be anticipated by the congregation as the time rolls around.

At our church we take Communion to all of our sick and shut-in members on the first Sunday of May and the first Sunday of October. Since we observe Communion on a monthly basis, shepherding deacons may take Communion to some of their sheep many more times a year than those two Sundays. The power of what we call worldwide Communion is that every sick and shut-in member of the church receives Communion on the same day. The list of those who are to receive Communion is placed in the weekly bulletin for two weeks in advance. Church members are invited to review the list to be sure that no one known to them as a sick or shut-in member is being overlooked or left out. On the designated days, the deacons go out two by two in every direction to deliver Communion to their brothers and sisters in Christ who are confined.

The fellowship that marks these days begins long before the first person ever receives Communion at home or in a hospital. It begins at the church where a dinner is prepared for those who will be going out right after the worship service to serve Communion. A committee of church members is responsible for providing that meal. Members of the deacon board and their family members, the clergy of the church, and other invited guests share in a warm time of fellowship and community building inside the church.

At the end of that meal, the visitation assignments are handed out, a prayer is offered, and then an important second-circle ministry begins. Members of the church who are unable to get out to the church prepare themselves for a visit that will include receiving Communion. I have served Communion hundreds of times to persons who have been unable to get to the church to share in that observance. I have rarely done so when it did not result in joy and gratitude on the part of the recipient and deep satisfaction on my part for being able to say to those persons the special words spoken by Jesus, "This is my body broken for you. . . . This is my blood poured out for the forgiveness of sin."

Praying for One Another— Not every form of pastoral care involves hands-on activities. Another equally vital form by which we care for one another is found in 1 Thessalonians 5:25 and again in 2 Thessalonians 3:1, where Paul invites the church to pray for him and for those who are serving alongside him. "Pray for us" is an appeal for continued strength and boldness from the leader of the entire Gentile church to its members in Thessalonica. Paul seemed to understand that the only way he could successfully do the work that was assigned to him was if his efforts were undergirded by the prayers of the people.

"Pray for us" was Paul giving expression to the clear realization that no ministry is accomplished entirely on the strength, ingenuity, training, financial resources, and/or experience of human beings. As Psalm 121:1-2 remind us, "I will lift up my eyes to the mountains—where does my help come from? My help comes from the LORD, the Maker of heaven and earth" (NIV). The church should not become so focused on programs and practices that could in many instances be provided by almost any social service agency that it loses sight of the energy and faith by which its work is supported. "Pray for us" is not something separate and apart from the physical ways by which Christians care for one another. "Pray for us" is a reminder that we are a distinctly Christian community with an interest in both body and soul. "Pray for us" reminds people who approach the church that Jesus fed the five thousand who gathered on a mountainside by the Sea of Galilee not as an event unto itself, but as part of a broader occasion when he was preaching about the values of the kingdom of God.

In truth, these words from Paul echo through the life of every Christian congregation around the world as members say to one another, "Pray for me." In the face of all of life's trials, there are people who are anxious to request and happy to receive the prayers of their fellow believers. One of the most comforting and reassuring things members within a local church can do is pray for one another. This is second-circle ministry at work: one Christian encouraging another through the power of intercessory prayer. A powerful spiritual community has been created when that spirit of praying for one another takes root in a congregation.

Like the apostle Paul, I have at times turned to the faith community with the words "Pray for me." I remember when I was initially diagnosed with prostate cancer. It was a devastating announcement that initially left me wondering how long I might have left to live. My response to that announcement, after simply reeling from the shock of the diagnosis, was to call people and urge them to pray for me. That request did not express a lack of faith in my surgeons or in their techniques or technology. I was simply acknowledging that my life was not entirely in the hands of doctors, nurses, catheter bags, and recovery techniques.

I went into my surgery under the watchful care of a Great Physician and surrounded by the prayers of other believers whose faith in God was as great as my own. Members of the church came to the hospital on the day of my surgery and sat with my family throughout the entire process. Others were praying throughout the day as they turned their attention and their faith in my direction. I specifically requested the prayers of the people, and I credit my recovery from cancer, in large measure, to the power of prayer. I absolutely believe in the words of James 5:13-16: "Are any among you suffering? They should pray. Are any cheerful? They should sing songs of praise. Are any among you sick? They should call for the elders of the church and have them pray over them, anointing them with oil in the name of the Lord. The prayer of faith will save the sick, and the Lord will raise them up; and anyone who has committed sins will be forgiven....The prayer of the righteous is powerful and effective" (NRSV).

The designation of being a righteous person is in no way limited only to the clergy or to ordained lay leaders such as deacons in a Baptist church. Paul was not thinking only about the apostles when he made his appeal in Thessalonica. He was seeking prayer from within the second circle; he was asking other Christians to pray for him. The prayers of all righteous people are powerful and effective whether they are seated on the platform or in the pews.

There are many ways by which prayer can be used as a means of second-circle ministry within a local church. The church may have a time of testimony during which the names of the sick can be called out. Many churches have a list of those requesting prayer in their weekly bulletin. At Antioch we have prayer request cards placed in the back of each pew and in various locations throughout the church. Members are invited to write down prayer requests concerning themselves and other persons and problems about which they want the whole church to be prayerful. Those requests are given to the deacons and are read aloud at the Wednesday evening prayer meeting so that members of the church can pray for one another.

This matter of praying for one another is more urgent than the time we all spend praying for and about ourselves. Jesus tells us that God already knows our needs before we ask about them (Matthew 6:8). However, Jesus says something more: instead of worrying about the things we think we need, we should trust God for those things and give our attention to seeking the kingdom of God and his righteousness (Matthew 6:33). In other words, mature Christians and churches with strong second-circle of care ministries spend far more time praying for others than they do praying for themselves.

Bear One Another's Burdens— One more way local churches can serve as second-circle caregivers for one another involves what Paul refers to as "bear[ing] one another's burdens" (Galatians 6:2). This text must be approached carefully so as not to make the challenge too easy or uncomplicated. In Galatians 6:1, Paul has just spoken about a brother or sister who has been caught in a sin. Unlike those persons in Jerusalem who were ready to stone the woman taken in adultery in John 8:3, Paul calls on the church in Galatia to restore gently. Paul makes that point while also saying to his readers, "Take care that you yourselves are not tempted."

Bearing one another's burdens has physical as well as spiritual components. The church can pray for its members struggling with addictions to alcohol and drugs, and it can also host one or more groups of Alcoholics Anonymous. We can pray for children attending troubled school districts, and the church can also sponsor tutoring and mentoring programs for children in their immediate neighborhood. We can pray for persons in prison, and the church can also sponsor a prison ministry that sends some of its members into correctional institutions to do ministry while sponsoring at the church various support programs for the families of those who are incarcerated.

What the church does not want to do is fall victim to the implications of the following litany taken from an essay by James Cone in *The Pastor as Servant.*

I was hungry and you formed a humanities club and you discussed my hunger.

Thank you.

I was imprisoned and you crept off quietly to your chapel in the cellar and prayed for my release.

I was naked and in your mind you debated the morality of my appearance.

I was sick and you knelt and thanked God for your health.

I was homeless and you preached to me of the spiritual shelter of the love of God.

I was lonely and you left me alone to pray for me.

You seem so holy; so close to God.

But I'm still very hungry and lonely and cold.

So where have your prayers gone? What have they done? What does it profit a man to page through his book of prayers when the rest of the world is crying for his help?[3]

It bears mentioning that Paul says in the Galatians 6 passage that when we bear each other's burdens we are fulfilling the law of Christ (v. 2). For Paul the law of Christ is not fulfilled when we manage to keep ourselves from sinning, as if such a thing were even possible. Instead, we fulfill the law of Christ when we are willing to forgive, encourage, and restore to fellowship those who have sinned either against us or around us. We should do this, because this is exactly what God has done for us: forgiven our sins and restored us to fellowship. That is the message of the gospel song that says:

Amazing grace shall always be my song of praise,
For it was grace that bought my liberty.
I do not know just why He came to love me so;
He looked beyond my fault and saw my need.

I shall forever lift mine eyes to Calvary,
To view the cross where Jesus died for me.
How marvelous the grace that caught my falling soul;
He looked beyond my fault and saw my need.[4]

We bear one another's burdens in the local church when we embrace and encourage and support those who have sinned, rather than voting immediately to expel them from membership. We do this not because we take sin lightly; we do this because we know perfectly well that every one of us is capable of sin and that we have sinned and fallen short of the glory of God (Romans 3:23). If there is one place where people should be able to speak openly about their struggles with sin and temptation, it ought to be the church. Conversely, if and when people feel they cannot mention their sins in the company of their brothers and sisters in Christ, that church has ceased to be salt in the earth. That church has ceased to serve as the light of the world. That church "is no longer good for anything" and should be "thrown out and trampled underfoot" (Matthew 5:13, NIV).

J. Louis Martyn offered an insight into this passage by creating a fictional comment by Paul about a man named Dionysius. Paul says: "I know that in his addiction, Brother Dionysius has wronged several of you. Together with other members of the church, you are to restore him to his former condition in the community, doing so in full knowledge of the fact that you are as subject to missteps as he is."[5]

What a wonderful church it would be that encouraged and allowed for sinners in its midst to experience repentance, reformation, and reconciliation with God and with others. Such a church would, of course, also be marked by the humility that comes from knowing that "there but by the grace of God go I." The second circle of care is a place where we can, or should be able to, bear one another's burdens of sin.

William Barclay offered a somewhat different insight into this same passage when he said, "There is a kind of burden which falls on a man which comes from the chances and the changes of life. It comes to him from outside; some crisis, some emergency, some sorrow may descend upon him. It is fulfilling the law of Christ to help everyone who is up against it."[6]

Every church has members who are "up against it." They have been suddenly and traumatically impacted by "some crisis, some emergency or some sorrow that has descended upon them." What a comfort it is to know that they do not have to face those times alone; people in their local church will help them bear their burdens of sorrow.

The emergency may involve a child suddenly in trouble with the criminal justice system. It may be the slow but steady dissolution of a marriage that everyone thought would last forever. Maybe an automobile accident has left someone seriously injured or a house fire has left another person homeless and coping with the loss of everything they owned except the clothes on their backs. They may be "up against it" in terms of being laid off from a job or facing home foreclosure as a result of that sudden loss of steady work. The local church and the second circle of care in particular are never more needed than in times such as these. And when the second circle does come together to show care and concern for a member of the body of Christ, they are fulfilling the law of Christ.

Churches can establish grief support ministries to aid members as they deal with the death of loved ones. Our church has a marriage enrichment program that serves as a support for couples, both before marriage and after they say "I do," and can help them work out whatever problems and differences may exist between them. When long-term hospitalization is the issue, the help may take the form of relieving family members who feel they have to sit at the bedside of an ill loved one around the clock. Others in the church can share in that bedside vigil and give some relief to the immediate family. Still others can be sure that meals are prepared for those who are so busy caring for a sick or injured loved one that they have little if any time to provide a decent meal for themselves.

Caring for One Another Can Take Other Forms— In some instances, we bear each other's burdens at times when sin is not the problem from which people are recovering and when restoration from sin is not the role that the church is being invited to play. We can also show care for one another when we open the doors of our church or even of our homes to people who may find themselves temporarily homeless as a result of foreclosure, domestic violence, or loss of employment and income. We can do it when we help to replace clothes and household items for persons who have been impacted by fire, flood, or other forms of natural disaster. It can happen when one person is willing to stand with another while he or she is seeking to have a criminal record expunged, to have a child released from police custody, to work through a complicated financial problem, or to adjust to the news about a serious, even life-threatening medical condition.

Our world has witnessed a wide variety of ways in which we can bear one another's burdens. Following the horrific damage caused by tornadoes, floods, blizzards, hurricanes, earthquakes, and tsunamis, individual Christians and entire congregations spring into action providing everything from bottled water and blankets to clothing and hot meals, as well as alternative places in which to worship when entire churches were destroyed and volunteer labor to help with rebuilding.

I personally saw one form by which church members practiced this principle of bearing one another's burdens in our church. Between 2009 and 2010, two members of our congregation faced the devastation of having fire consume the places in which they lived. In both instances, everything they owned was destroyed by fire. Their loss was obviously devastating, but they did not have to wait long to feel the warm and caring embrace of their congregation. Food, clothing, cash gifts, offers of a place to live, and the offer of assistance in a dozen other ways emerged from every direction. Nothing could undo the loss each of them had sustained, but they were greatly aided through their respective times of crisis because there were so many people in their church willing to help them bear their burdens.

The notion that the second circle of care is a sign of a strong church is echoed in the following observation by Roger Kruger. In writing about the way in which he and his local church were called on to bear the burdens of one of the members of their congregation, he made the following point: "Involvement in congregational life develops an awareness of our interrelatedness and interdependence.... Congregations have their problems...but within congregations we have the opportunity to learn from others, to join with others in searching for solutions, and to practice sacrificial living that benefits community. I am rediscovering the value of being 'religious,' of renewing a commitment that binds me to others as well as to God."[7]

Congregations are not simply people who happen to worship together for an hour or two each Sunday morning. Congregations that have been equipped by a caring pastor to do the work of the ministry will become the setting for a second circle of care in which members show care and concern for one another.

Notes

1. Liston Pope, quoted in David M. Reimers, *White Protestantism and the Negro* (New York: Oxford, 1965), 186.

2. Seward Hiltner, *The Christian Shepherd: Some Aspects of Pastoral Care* (Nashville: Abingdon, 1959), 14.

3. Earl Shelp and Ronald H. Sunderland, eds., *The Pastor as Servant* (New York: Pilgrim, 1986), 63–64.

4. Dottie Rambo, "He Looked beyond My Fault," in *African American Heritage Hymnal* (Chicago: GIA Publications, 2001), 249–50.

5. J. Louis Martyn, *Galatians*. Anchor Bible, vol. 33A (New York: Doubleday, 1997), 547.

6. William Barclay, *The Letters to the Galatians and Ephesians* (Philadelphia: Westminster, 1958), 58.

7. Roger Kruger, "Penalized," *Christian Century*, December 14, 2010, 11.

Second-Circle Questions for Consideration

1. In what ways does your church practice the principle of "bear[ing] one another's burdens" as stated in Galatians 6:2?

2. Is intercessory prayer an important part of the life of your congregation? If so, in what ways is it facilitated?

3. Does your church have a regular methodology by which sick and shut-in members of the congregation receive a visit or a greeting?

4. In what ways do lay leaders (nonclergy persons) aid in providing various expressions of care for members of the congregation?

5. Do you think it is important to make some second-circle forms of ministry a line item in the annual budget of your church?

6. What spiritual attributes should lay leaders possess if they want to be involved in second-circle forms of care?

7. In what ways are all of the issues discussed in Acts 6:1-16 important for twenty-first-century churches?

8. Who are the people that play the role of Aaron and Hur (Exodus 17:8-13) in your congregation? Is this a role you would be willing to play?

9. Have you ever offered yourself as a resource to someone who is presently facing a problem or circumstance you had earlier encountered?

10. Using Mark 2 as our example, how far would you be willing to go to demonstrate care and concern for someone in your congregation? Would you expect or desire any credit or recognition beyond their gratitude for any service you rendered to that person?

The Third Circle—The Congregation in Community

CHAPTER 10

Developing a Third Circle of Pastoral Care

"You are the salt of the earth. . . . You are
the light of the world."
—Matthew 5:13-14

Thus far in this book we have developed a model of pastoral care within the local church that is delivered through the image of three concentric circles of activity. The first circle of care involves a caring pastor operating out of a shepherding motif and working to transform his or her congregation into a community of caring people. Within such a community, members care for one another in times of crisis or need. That is the second circle. In this and the following chapters, we will see this caring community move into the third circle, beyond the doors of the church, to care for those outside the church family.

How Far Should Caring People Extend Their Love and Concern?
How far should the care and concern of any congregation be extended? Does our discipleship extend only as far as our membership, or are we also called to care for those beyond our church walls? Clearly the Great Commission sends us beyond ourselves—beyond Jerusalem (our own faith community) to Judea and

Samaria (the neighboring communities, both like and unlike ourselves)—and even to the ends of the earth (see Acts 1:8).

The question of how far we reach with ministries of pastoral care
leads us to the third circle of care, which involves a congregation
that extends itself outward, beyond the walls of its sanctuary and
beyond the names on its membership rolls. The third circle of care
is what drives a congregation to seek opportunities to touch the
people and address the problems outside its church doors. Here
again the movement of care and concern is outward—outward
from the pastor to the congregation, outward from one member of
the congregation to another, and now outward from the congregation to its immediate neighborhood or environs and even to the
wider world.

Please don't dismiss this idea as some secular form of social
activism or community outreach unrelated to the work of ministry and disconnected from the task of pastoral care. On the contrary, the third circle may be considered the highest form of pastoral care, because it pushes the love and concern that disciples
should have for one another outward in a way that encourages
and equips those disciples to show a similar love and concern for
the people who live and work nearby. The Great Commandment
to love your neighbor as you love yourself (Leviticus 19:18;
Matthew 19:19) cannot be limited to the neighbors who are seated in the pews next to you.

"Who Is My Neighbor?"

In Luke 10:25-37, an expert in the law of Moses identified the idea
of love of one's neighbor as the foundation for gaining eternal life.
However, when he pressed Jesus about whom he should consider
to be his neighbor, Jesus shocked his listeners by telling the parable
of the good Samaritan. If ever there was an oxymoron in first-century Israel, the idea of a "good Samaritan" would certainly have
qualified. Jews despised Samaritans and would never have viewed

them as neighbors to be loved according to the law of Moses. Yet in Jesus' parable, a Samaritan was the one good enough to demonstrate love and care for a beaten and dying man on the road between Jerusalem and Jericho.

That honor could have fallen to a Jewish priest or a Levite, two men who could well have been considered neighbors of the beaten man and who certainly would have known and honored the Law. However, for reasons that may have involved ritual cleanliness or the urgency of professional ministerial duties, those religious leaders did not get involved with their countryman. The stranger, the outsider, "the other," was the one who displayed the traits of neighborliness, and Jesus concluded his tale by telling that expert in the Law of Moses to "go and do likewise."

In Matthew 25:35 and 43, Jesus referred to how we will all be judged based on how we treat strangers and "the least of these." As Jesus' disciples, we cannot reserve our love and care only for those persons who are known to us or who are institutionally connected to us in one way or another. True Christian love, love for one's neighbor, should move us, as if in concentric circles, in a consistently outward direction so that we can impact and improve the lives of the people who may not be members of our churches, but who are members of the communities in which our churches are situated.

The Danger of Being an Introverted Church

In an earlier chapter, I cited James Harris of Virginia Union University who issued a warning about what he calls "introverted churches," those whose congregations are focused on the worship life that takes place inside their sanctuaries and unconcerned about the work they could and should be doing in the community that surrounds their church building. Harris argues that churches must "move beyond personal conversion to community transformation."[1] That movement is exactly what occurs with the outward effects of the third circle of care: people who have been converted and transformed by their faith in Christ will display their faith by the love and concern they have for others, both inside the church and beyond its walls.

For Harris, something great is at stake when introverted churches remain detached from the communities outside their doors. The reign of God throughout the world is inhibited when the church, the entity meant to be the light of the world, hides its light under a basket by remaining focused only on activities that occur within its walls. The church must be engaged with its community. In fact, Harris goes on to say: "The concept of community needs to be expanded to include the whole community—the church and the world. However, as long as the church is introverted and parochial in its approach to ministry, it will continue in its failure to effect liberation and change in the United States and the world."[2]

Lessons from the Dead Sea

We can learn an important lesson about church life by considering the geography and topography of Israel. By watching the movement of water from the Sea of Galilee in the northern part of the country down to the Dead Sea far in the south, we learn about the power of moving outward—and the dangers of not doing so. The Sea of Galilee is a body of freshwater that feeds into the Jordan River in a downhill pattern. That freshwater makes irrigation possible, allowing animal, plant, and human life to thrive in that country. There can be no doubt that the Sea of Galilee and the Jordan River are as central to the life of Israel as the Nile River is to Egypt or the Mississippi River is to many states in this country. The key to such life-giving power is that freshwater flows outward and throughout the heart of the land.

Now consider the fact that the freshwater of the Sea of Galilee flows through the Jordan River until it arrives at what is called the Dead Sea or the Salt Sea. At that point, the water settles into a place that is below sea level, in the middle of a barren desert area, where the freshwater has nowhere else to flow, so it becomes stagnant and lifeless. Nothing can grow around the Dead Sea, and nothing can live in the Dead Sea. When the water stops flowing, death quickly ensues. The water that has flowed in does not flow through, and so it breeds death and not life.

The Dead Sea, which is not actually a sea at all but a landlocked lake between Israel and Jordan, is the lowest body of water on earth at approximately 1,296 feet (395 meters) below sea level.[3] The name Dead Sea comes from the fact that many millennia ago a stream of thick sediment, including shale, clay, sandstone, rock, and salt, was deposited on existing layers of sand and gravel. This millennium-long accumulation of sediment, combined with the desert climate and water heated by thermal sulfur springs to a year-round temperature of 72 degrees Fahrenheit, creates an extraordinarily high level of saline in the water.[4] However, it is not the salt content that makes the sea "dead" but its stagnancy and the barren surroundings. Nothing can grow in or near that body of water.

If the waters of the Jordan could pass through the Dead Sea, it is very likely that over time the heavy sediment could be washed away and the sea could breed life. That is what happened with the BP oil spill in the Gulf of Mexico in 2010 and with the Exxon Valdez oil spill in Alaska many years earlier. The waters that kept flowing were able to break up the thick, heavy oil and restore life to those damaged bodies of water.

Something similar can happen in our churches. Imagine the freshwater of the gospel and the good news of Jesus Christ regularly flowing into the church, bringing life-giving and life-changing power. Every time the members of the church gather for worship, there is the possibility of something fresh and revitalizing flowing from the Spirit of Christ into their churches, resulting in new members, new programs, and a fresh new Word that can offer new inspiration for the congregation. Every Sunday becomes another occasion when the church can be challenged, refreshed, and equipped.

This is especially important when people come to church after a long week where they have been exposed to the values, vocabulary, and venomous behavior of people on their job, in their community, and even in their family that are radically out of step with the message of the gospel and the reign of God that stand at the heart of the biblical story. Like a thorough watering that restores life to drooping plants, the fresh Word that is preached or taught can become living water for thirsty souls.[5]

However, because so many churches are introverted, the words of life that flow into them on Sunday morning do not keep flowing outward—sometimes not even reaching the parking lot or surrounding streets, and certainly not flowing into the workweek or the neighborhoods and businesses beyond the walls of the church. Instead, like the water in the Dead Sea, the words of life that flowed into the church do not move outward into the community. As a result, the words of life and the witness of the church become stagnant and no longer create or sustain life.

The Church Must Send Out as Much as It Takes In

Informed by the image of the life-giving waters from the Sea of Galilee and the contrast of what happens when that freshwater empties into the Dead Sea where it grows stagnant and lifeless, we must understand that the movement from the second circle of care where church members care for one another *must* flow outward into the third circle of care where the church reaches out to show concern for people beyond its walls. Failure to do so is not only to deny life-giving waters to the community, but also to cause the church itself to become a stale environment where nothing can live.

In other words, the third circle of care is important not only for the good of the community that is recipient of the church's acts of love and concern; it is just as vital for the church itself, because we need the outlet by which the grace that has flowed into our life together can flow through us and on to others. The third circle of care is the means by which the church fulfills its ministry as dramatically set forth in Matthew 25:31-46. At the same time, it is the form of pastoral care by which the lives of people who reside outside the walls of our local churches can be blessed and empowered by those who are willing to let the love of God flow through them and into the lives of others.

What a terrifying thought to imagine churches that are more like the Dead Sea than like the fresh and life-giving Sea of Galilee—all because they refuse to allow life to flow through them to the people and problems just beyond their doors. Every church would benefit from assessing its present ministry with this analogy in mind. The issue is not what flows into the church in terms of new members or increased tithes and offerings. The issue is what flows out from the church into the surrounding community and the wider world—through ministries of discipleship, transformation, justice, and care.

The Dead Sea cannot be blamed for having no outlet for the freshwater that flows into its basin; topography in Israel cannot be reversed. But local churches can and will be held accountable if the fresh resources that flow into them get bottled up and do not flow through to refresh and enrich the lives of the people just outside our doors.

Saving Souls Is the Beginning, Not the End

I have heard too many pastors disavow any interest in ministries that might fall within the third circle of pastoral care (i.e., ministries for the wider community) on the grounds that they are in the "soul-saving business." Their assumption seems to be that saving souls inside the church and working to save the quality of life for people outside the church are antithetical or incompatible. Some pastors see the work of evangelism (saving souls) as having nothing to do with the work of social justice or societal transformation.

But let us ask ourselves what people should be doing after they have been saved. If personal salvation from sin and its consequences is the be all and end all of our faith, then what does God expect us to do from the moment of our conversion until the day of our death? Shouldn't the same pastor who was instrumental in leading people to a saving knowledge of Jesus Christ also be the pastor who challenges and motivates those "saved" persons onward to the work of discipleship and service in the name of the Lord who set them free from sin?

In Christian theology, there is no works righteousness through which we can work for or earn our salvation. No magical number of good deeds performed over any prescribed period of time can secure our souls against the wages of sin. Paul made that abundantly clear in Ephesians 2:8-10 when he made two important points. First he said, "For it is by grace you have been saved, through faith—and this is not from yourselves, it is the gift of God—not by works, so that no one can boast" (vv. 8-9, NIV). But having acknowledged that we need to be saved and having stated that our salvation is accomplished by faith and not by works, Paul went on to speak about what the saints should be doing after being saved by grace. To that end he says: "For we are God's handiwork, created in Christ Jesus to do good works, which God prepared in advance for us to do" (v. 10, NIV).

While evangelism and church growth should not be the first priority or ulterior motive for pastoral care ministries, the goals of saving souls and nurturing disciples won't suffer when churches establish second- (and third-) circle care ministries. Spiritual conversions and church growth often occur as individuals and communities are touched and transformed through ministries of love and concern. Rusaw and Swanson affirm the interface between evangelism and service: "One of the most effective ways to reach people with the message of Jesus Christ today is through real and relevant acts of service. Honest, compassionate service can restore credibility to the crucial message we have to share. To tell the truth, we must show the truth. It's the model Jesus used. He served. He met needs. People listened."[6]

Paul Nixon issues a stern challenge to any church that refuses to follow the example of Jesus in serving the needs of the people that live within its surrounding neighborhood. He says, "If a church is unwilling or unable to minister to the people who live near its facility, it should prayerfully consider relocating and offering that facility to a group who is committed to serving the neighborhood."[7] Churches that sit empty and idle during the week and only open so members can come in and worship do not honor the God they have gathered to worship, and they are not obeying the teachings of the God whose commandments they claim to have embraced.

I would take Nixon's challenge a step further. Churches that are not willing to minister in the areas where they are presently located should not simply relocate so they can continue to be inactive, inaccessible, and irrelevant in some other neighborhood. Such churches should prayerfully consider shutting down altogether. It is likely that no one but their membership will miss them when they are gone.

Faith without Works Is Still Dead

Those who attempt to separate the work of salvation from the work of discipleship and service will have a difficult time getting around the words of James: "What good is it, my brothers and sisters, if you say you have faith but do not have works? Can faith save you? If a brother or sister is naked and lacks daily food, and one of you says to them, 'Go in peace; keep warm and eat your fill,' and yet you do not supply their bodily needs, what is the good of that? So faith by itself, if it has no works is dead" (2:14-17).

The third circle of care is the means and method by which we fulfill this mandate of the whole gospel—the gospel that James and Paul preached, whereby we act out our faith through service, generosity, love, and compassion, and the gospel that Jesus proclaimed in Matthew 25, wherein our integrity and authenticity as followers of Christ will be judged by how we treat those the world deems "least." Thus, the faith that saves us also empowers and equips us to go out and show God's love and concern for those people and problems that reside just outside the doors of our local churches.

Let us be clear, however. What occurs in the third circle of care is not necessarily based on or hopeful of any evangelistic outcomes. The goal of the third circle is not church growth but Christian witness. What is at stake is not enlarging our membership rolls but showing compassion toward people who need to feel the love of God's people in a tangible way. Third-circle care is not merely a means to an end. It is a gospel work in and of itself.

Jesus never required conversion as a prerequisite for those he healed or fed or raised from the dead. He never invited them to "join the church" before he unleashed the power of the Spirit. Rather, in the words of Acts 10:37-38: "You know what has happened throughout the province of Judea, beginning in Galilee after the baptism that John preached—how God anointed Jesus of Nazareth with the Holy Spirit and power, and how he went around doing good and healing all who were under the power of the devil, because God was with him" (NIV). That is how the local church should work in its community and in the world; once we have been baptized, we too should go around doing good in the name and power of Jesus.

Doing Good and Coming Glory

The quote from Acts 10:37-38 and the phrase "[Jesus] went around doing good" bring to mind a beautiful hymn I hear primarily in

African American churches. Among the lines of that hymn are these words: "Doing good deeds, sowing good seeds, That's how I want the Lord to find me."[8]

Inherent in this hymn are two points that bear further analysis. First is the phrase "doing good deeds." Personal salvation that does not lead into a ministry of service and caring in the name of the one who has saved us is an altogether inadequate response to the grace that has been showered upon us. The Lord who saves us wants to be able to send us into the vineyard to labor on God's behalf. The third circle of care reminds us of that fact, and it also serves to facilitate and institutionalize that activity. What is at stake here is where those good deeds must be performed. Can we limit ourselves only to what we do within the context of our local church and its membership? Does Jesus not also call us to step out and offer our "good deeds"—our acts of service and care—beyond the walls of the church and into the wider community?

The second issue raised by the hymn is captured in the lyric "That's how I want the Lord to find me." This phrase speaks of accountability, consequences, judgment, and that fateful day when the Son of Man comes in glory. On that day, each of us will be required to stand in the presence of a holy God who will consider whether we have been faithful disciples of Jesus Christ. We would do well to remember the great judgment scene in Matthew 25:31-46 and the types of people with whom Jesus identifies himself—the hungry, the poor, the naked, the incarcerated. How can we possibly address all of those areas of responsibility and accountability while remaining safely within the walls of our church sanctuaries and fellowship halls? If we want the Lord to find us faithful, let us avoid the peril of becoming or remaining a Dead Sea church and grasp the urgency of allowing Christ's living water to flow through our ministry and witness beyond the walls of our churches and into the world around us.

Notes

1. James Henry Harris, *Pastoral Theology: A Black Church Perspective* (Minneapolis: Fortress, 1991), 34.

2. Harris, 35.

3. W. H. Morton, s.v., "Dead Sea," *Interpreter's Dictionary of the Bible* (Nashville: Abingdon, 1962), 1:788–89.

4. Morton, 789.

5. This phrase is borrowed from Marvin McMickle, *Living Water for Thirsty Souls: Unleashing the Power of Exegetical Preaching* (Valley Forge, PA: Judson Press, 2001).

6. Rick Rusaw and Eric Swanson, *The Externally Focused Church* (Loveland, CO: Group, 2004), 11.

7. Paul Nixon, *Fling Open the Doors: Giving the Church Away to the Community* (Nashville: Abingdon, 2002), 23.

8. Alma Androzzo and Virginia Davis, "How I Want the Lord to Find Me," in *Singspiration* (Chicago: GIA Publications, 1964), 68.

CHAPTER 11

A Caring Church Is a Living Church

"You have a name of being alive, but you are dead.
Wake up, and strengthen what remains
and is on the point of death."
—Revelation 3:1-2

In 2010 Princeton University professor Eddie Glaude Jr. caused a surge of outrage in the African American Christian community when he wrote, "The black church is dead."[1] Despite the criticism he faced for his choice of words, Glaude was making a point that is pertinent to our discussion about a third circle of care. After shocking readers with his initial statement, he acknowledged that black churches continue to exist in great numbers; he was not suggesting, therefore, that African American congregations had become extinct. Rather, Glaude was mourning what he perceived to be the death of influence and relevance among a once thriving and engaged faith community. He declared that "the idea of this venerable institution as central to black life and as a repository for a social and moral conscience for the nation has all but disappeared."[2] He observed a trend toward an inward focus on matters that concern no one but the members of the congregation.

Like the biblical prophets, Glaude mingled anger with hope and the possibility that this death could be defeated in a resurrection of new life. He had no desire to preach a eulogy for the black church; he used strong language to sound a call to renewal—and to renewed focus on matters beyond congregational life. He said:

> The death of the black church as we have known it occasions an opportunity to breathe new life into what it means to be black and Christian. Black churches and preachers must find their prophetic voices in this momentous present moment. And in doing so, black churches will rise again and insist that we all assert ourselves on the national stage not as sycophants to a glorious past, but as witnesses to the ongoing revelation of God's love in the here and now as we work on behalf of those who suffer most.[3]

In truth, Glaude's concern about the black church can transfer to a concern about the role and relevance of any and all churches in the twenty-first century. The black church is not alone in spending too much time looking in the rearview mirror and remembering its golden age. Most Christian churches in North America are engrossed in the same anguished exercise. Society continues to make choices and shape policy every day, and for the most part does so on the basis of socioeconomic, political, ideological, and ethnic-cultural considerations—but largely without much reference to the church.

Most persons would readily agree that the church universal in this nation has ceased to be the "social and moral conscience for the nation."[4] We are welcome to make our pronouncements about right and wrong within the walls of our church buildings, but our voice has become unfamiliar and even unwanted when brought to issues in the public square. Nevertheless, it is not too late to reinsert the voice of the church and the ministry of the church back into the life of the world outside our doors.

Where Is Our Focus?

We have considered the analogy of the life-giving waters of Galilee and the Jordan in contrast with the stagnant waters of the Dead Sea as an illustration of why we need the third concentric circle of pastoral care. Others have suggested a different perspective to help churches and pastors think about that outward reach of Christian disciples.

In their book *The Externally Focused Church*, Rick Rusaw and Eric Swanson use the phrase "externally focused church." They offer this description: "Externally focused churches are convinced that good deeds and good news can't and shouldn't be separated. Just as it takes two wings to lift an airplane off the ground, so externally focused churches couple good news with good deeds to make an impact on their communities. The good deed, expressed in service and ministry to others, validates the good news. The good news explains the purpose of the good deeds."[5] Rusaw and Swanson argue that an external focus must be at the core of a congregation's identity. In other words, reaching out to the community cannot be something that is done from time to time or every now and then. They say, "Externally focused churches have concluded that it's really not church if it's not engaged in the life of the community through ministry and service to others."[6] They press the importance of having a constant focus on outreach by saying, "An external focus is embedded in their DNA."[7] Or to return to our concentric circles model, pastoral care ought to ripple out naturally from clergy to congregation to community, and the gospel message is the stone that sends out those ripples of good deeds. Acts of service, outreach, advocacy, and compassion are the natural overflow of the church's identity as a community of caring people.

Becoming a Village Church

Many people are familiar with the African proverb (popularized by Marian Wright Edelman and the Children's Defense Fund) "It takes a village to raise a child." The idea behind that proverb is that children are best served when everyone in the community contributes something to their growth and development. Parents cannot do the job of raising a child alone; the task takes a village. What if that African proverb were reworked to describe a vital relationship between the church and healthy families and communities?

Author Paul Nixon, in *Fling Open the Doors: Giving the Church Away to the Community*, suggests the term "village church"[8] as a model for increasing the Christian church's relevance and engagement with the world beyond. "Village church" offers a kind of complementary paradigm to the previous models of ensuring a third circle of pastoral care in an externally focused congregation. In a village church, the congregation sees itself as a natural and even an essential part of the community in which it is situated. Instead of holding a traditional worship service in the comfort and confines of its own four walls while waiting for members of the community to come to it, a village church flings open its doors, creating traffic in two directions. Not only are church members going out into the community, but the community begins coming into the church.

Nixon states unequivocally: "The members of the village church understand that the church exists for the community and belongs to the community. In fact, they consider it a sacred responsibility to serve the people who live in their community....The territory involved can be a neighborhood or an entire city: it is simply the geographic area for which the church takes special responsibility."[9] Nixon argues that it is possible to measure whether a congregation has reached the status of being a village church. "Once the church understands that it belongs to the community, the community itself will begin to figure this out as well."[10] Real estate agents will refer newcomers to the church based on its reputation in the community. Local psychologists and medical providers will encourage clients to visit based on reports of how the congregation cares for people's practical as well as spiritual needs. Community groups looking for a place to meet will call on a village church that is known for its hospitality and lavish welcome for outsiders. All these are also ripples in the third circle of care.

Lessons from the Lord

What about Nixon's point that a village church is defined by the geographical area for which the church takes special responsibility? What is involved in taking responsibility for a neighborhood, a town, or a city? For one, a local church must be undeterred in any way from reaching out into that community no matter what cultural or ethnic traditions or differences may separate the members of the congregation from the members of the area in question. Jesus offers us some valuable lessons in looking beyond cultural and ethnic differences.

A theological thread runs through the gospel narratives involving Jesus and various groups of Gentiles or other "outsiders." Each encounter that Jesus had with such a person should be noted, because in each case an important lesson is being taught about how disciples of Jesus should view and respond to people who might otherwise be perceived as being outside our normal circle of care and concern. As we will see, Jesus was always doing ministry in an outward direction.

A Samaritan Woman— We begin with John 4:9 where Jesus is asking a Samaritan woman to give him a drink from the well. It would have been shocking enough that Jesus would let himself be seen talking openly with any woman. That was a serious breach of first-century social protocol, given the low social status women endured in that time and place. Thus, when the disciples entered the scene, they "were surprised to find him talking with a woman" (John 4:27, NIV).

However, there was an even broader and deeper chasm that Jesus was crossing than that which involved gender roles in first-century Palestine. The real issue was that Jesus was talking with a Samaritan woman, someone who was far outside of any claim to the Jewish Jesus' care or concern. The Samaritan woman herself was surprised that Jesus addressed her. "'You are a Jew and I am a Samaritan woman. How can you ask me for a drink?' (For Jews do not associate with Samaritans)" (John 4:9, NIV).

The chasm between Jews and Samaritans was hundreds of years old and dated back to the destruction of the northern kingdom of Israel by the Assyrians in 722 BC. The Assyrians sent into exile throughout their vast empire many members of the Jewish ruling class as well as many artisans and craftsmen. At the same time, they relocated persons from other parts of their empire into northern Israel where they eventually mingled with the thousands of peasants who had not been deported (see Ezra 4:2). This resulted in a mixed race that did not meet the standards of racial or religious purity in the eyes of Jews who had not been subjected to that experience.

To make matters worse, the Samaritans in the northern part of Israel set up a religious system that was decidedly different from what took place in the temple in Jerusalem. They erected their own temple on Mount Gerizim. They limited their sacred Scriptures to the Pentateuch alone, not embracing the Hebrew prophets or the rest of what is known as the Hebrew Bible. These factors created irreconcilable differences between Jews and Samaritans.

Not only was the woman Jesus met at the well a Samaritan, but she had lived a less than ideal lifestyle. She had been married many times before, and as Jesus seemed to know already, the man she was currently living with was not her husband. The woman does not offer an explanation for her past, nor does Jesus seem to require one. His knowledge was sufficient to warrant her response: "Sir, I can see that you are a prophet" (John 4:19, NIV).

We do know that this woman was drawing her water alone at the noon hour, in contrast with the custom of gathering water early, before the sun grew hot. It seems likely that her history, whatever it was, may have made her feel unwelcome in the company of other women. She was certainly made to feel unwanted by the disciples when they found Jesus speaking with her (John 4:27). The only person who did not make her feel unwanted was Jesus. Note this encounter: the Son of God engaged in a pastoral moment with a scandalous Samaritan woman.

In many churches today, any one of those issues would be enough to prevent church members from reaching out and engaging with such a person. Some congregations might not want to deal with people of "ill repute." Others are so gender conscious they may not want to engage women as peers in any way. Some congregations have been known to resist all attempts at diversity within their congregation, and even move out of the neighborhood where their church has stood for decades when other ethnic groups begin to move in. Still other churches have chosen to close down altogether rather than undergo racial and cultural integration or transition.

I saw a recent report about a church in Brooklyn, New York, that houses two distinct ethnic congregations: one Latino and one Chinese.[11] The Sunset Park United Methodist Church was originally built to serve a Norwegian congregation. When the Norwegians moved out, the Latinos moved into the building. Today a congregation of thirty Latinos shares the church building with a Chinese congregation that has grown to over a thousand members. However, all the two churches seem to share is the church building. The report in the *New York Times* began with this description: "Two pastors preach from the same pulpit and live in the same parsonage next door, but they are barely on speaking terms and openly criticize each other's approach to the faith. In the church's social hall, two camps eye each other suspiciously as one finishes its meal of rice and beans while the other prepares steaming pans of chicken lo mein....This season there are even competing Christmas trees."[12]

Here is a case where care and concern are absent even among two Christian congregations that share the same building, largely because each views the other as "the stranger." That is only a small example of how easy it is for churches to withhold concern from people whose existence occurs entirely outside the life of any congregation simply because those people are viewed as strangers.

What Jesus did in John 4:4-30 was to take away our right to close our eyes, our hearts, and our resources to people who reside outside our congregational life. Jesus engaged a Samaritan woman in open dialogue, and she eventually invited her entire village to come and encounter Jesus for themselves. This was not social activism or community outreach; this was an example of third-circle pastoral care, a Jewish rabbi reaching out to an individual outside his own community of disciples—an act that resulted in an evangelistic experience for an entire town. By accepting the Samaritan village's offer of hospitality (unthinkable for any Jew, much less a rabbi and his disciples!), Jesus challenged his disciples then and the church today to engage in third-circle pastoral care—and to accept the two-way traffic that is the natural result.

When Jesus opened the door to dialogue, the community opened its doors in response. When Christ's living water poured into that village, they also had the opportunity to pour into the lives of Jesus and his followers. An entire Samaritan community confessed that Jesus was the Savior of the world after he had accepted their invitation to stay with them, which he did for two days (John 4:40). Seven hundred years of animosity and division were undone solely as a result of Jesus reaching beyond the borders and boundaries of his Jewish world to engage with Samaritans in an act of third-circle pastoral care.

A Canaanite Woman— In Matthew 15:21-28 Jesus is challenged by a person from outside his community to share care and concern for an outsider. A Canaanite woman from the region of Tyre and Sidon in Lebanon approached Jesus on behalf of her daughter, whom she believed to be demon-possessed. Despite the woman's urgent pleas, Jesus did not answer her or acknowledge her in any way. Finally, his disciples urged him to respond: "Send her away, for she keeps crying out after us" (v. 23, NIV). Denying any responsibility for her plight or appeal, Jesus told her in typical first-century Palestinian terms, "I was sent only to the lost sheep of Israel....It is not right to take the children's bread and toss it to the dogs" (vv. 24, 26, NIV).

With that one statement, seven hundred years of distinction between Jews and Gentiles rose up as an obstacle between Jesus and this needy woman. If the story had ended with that comment, it might be difficult to pursue the idea of the third-circle of care. After all, this was *Jesus* declaring that he had no obligation to those who were not members of his family of faith. But this woman was not so easily denied. She did not seek to refute Jesus' statement or to assert herself as his equal. She took another approach altogether, the path of humility, a path that Jesus could not resist. She said, "Yes it is, Lord. Even the dogs eat the crumbs that fall from their master's table" (v. 27, NIV). With that comment, Jesus' heart was moved, and her daughter was immediately healed.

At one point in his life then, even Jesus was content to limit his care and concern to those who were members of his own ethnic and faith community. His disciples encouraged him to send the woman away, and unlike his choice in John 4, this time Jesus seemed to agree with his disciples and verbally pushes the stranger away. However, when the woman dared to persist and cried out humbly for his intervention, Jesus set aside ancient prejudices and differences and responded to her legitimate need as one human being to another.

Jesus in the Synagogue in Nazareth— One of the most revealing stories about how people of faith in the Bible viewed those outside the walls of their community is found in Luke 4:23-30. In this text, Jesus recalls two stories from the Hebrew Scriptures—one about the Syrophoenician widow who was visited by the prophet Elijah, and the other about the Syrian leper named Naaman who was healed by the prophet Elisha. Earlier in this chapter of Luke, Jesus had read from the scroll of Isaiah and appeared to declare himself to be the long-awaited Messiah whose appearance would mark the fulfillment of that prophecy. After that shocking declaration made by a hometown boy in the very synagogue where he had grown up, the response of the community was surprisingly calm. Luke 4:22 says, "All spoke well of him and were amazed at the gracious words that came from his lips" (NIV). Their comments seem to carry the sense of "hometown boy makes good."

That sense of affirmation and affection is quickly transformed into a sense of rage and condemnation. Why? Because Jesus dared to suggest that the love of God, which all residents of Nazareth would assume as their birthright, was extended in equal measure to persons who resided well outside their community. Jesus told them that there were many widows in Israel during the days of the prophet Elijah. However, as recorded in 1 Kings 17:7-24, God directed Elijah to a widow in Zarephath, which was a region near the city of Sidon (modern-day Lebanon). Jesus went on to point out that while there were many lepers in Israel during the time of the prophet Elisha, the healing power of God had been reserved for a Gentile named Naaman, the leprous general of the Syrian army (2 Kings 5:1-15).

The very idea that "our God" could also show love, care, and concern for "those people" was more than the people of Nazareth could accept. Jesus seemed to be suggesting that the God of Abraham, Isaac, and Jacob was also the God of the Gentiles—of the foreigners, the strangers, the outsiders. Apparently the prospect of being asked to share their God with Gentiles was less acceptable to the people of Nazareth than hearing the one they knew as "Joseph's son" hailing himself as Messiah. You might have thought that they would stone Jesus for blasphemy when he claimed that the prophecy of Isaiah was fulfilled by his coming. Instead, the people wanted to throw Jesus off a mountain cliff only when he told them that God's love was broad enough to include those outside their community of faith (Luke 4:28-29).

Despite the reaction of others (then and now) to Jesus' message, that is the message that demands our attention. The love of God is not limited to or restricted to the members of our faith community. God's love and care extend beyond those walls into the lives and needs of those persons whom we might be inclined to overlook or undervalue simply because they are not "one of us." Rather than rejecting any reminder that the love of God reaches beyond us to those who reside just outside our doors, we should be like Elijah and Elisha who came to the aid of strangers, and in doing so revealed what it means to be true followers of God. That is what the third circle of pastoral care does; it allows us to follow God in expressing our love and concern for people who may not be a part of our congregation but who are a part of our community.

A Roman Centurion— In Matthew 8:5-13, Jesus encountered someone else whose request a Jewish rabbi would certainly have ignored: a Roman centurion. This man surely represented the ultimate outsider—the conqueror whose army was now occupying the land of Israel. But the encounter proved to be full of surprises.

The centurion approached Jesus on behalf of a servant who was sick and suffering at the centurion's home. Without waiting to be asked, Jesus agreed to accompany that Roman centurion home: "I will come and cure him." The text does not suggest that the servant in question was Jewish and that therefore Jesus was only caring for someone within his ethnic and faith community. The servant of a Roman centurion could have come from any of the nations that were under Roman rule. Thus, nothing indicates that Jesus' willingness was based on a first-circle relationship of care. In fact, the story soon clarifies that the relationship was not an insider one at all.

The centurion had a surprise of his own when he declined Jesus' offer to go to the house where the servant lay ill. The centurion, it seemed, recognized something in Jesus that he knew from personal experience. Jesus also possessed authority, the Roman officer observed, so all the Lord needed to do was speak the words—give the order—and the centurion knew the healing was assured. Jesus exclaimed his own surprise: "Truly I tell you, in no one in Israel have I found such faith" (v. 10).

Perhaps the only thing greater than the faith of that centurion was the divide that Jesus crossed when he agreed to heal that servant—a vast ethnic, political, and religious divide. So we may still ask, how should modern churches respond to the presence of people just outside our doors? Prayerfully, the answer is that we will follow the example of our Lord who was ready without any hesitation to hear and respond to the concerns of a Roman centurion. Most churches will never have to reach that far beyond their own walls!

Zacchaeus, the Chief Tax Collector— The only type of person in all of Israel who might have been more hated or scorned than a Roman soldier was a tax collector like Zacchaeus, whose story is found in Luke 19. Tax collectors were hated because they were Jews who collected taxes on behalf of the Roman Empire. They were viewed as traitors for participating in the economic oppression that made possible Rome's occupation of and military reign over Israel. The status of tax collectors was made all the worse by the fact that tax collectors were allowed to keep for themselves whatever revenue they could generate beyond the amount they were required to turn over to Rome. (It is that work incentive Zacchaeus referenced in verse 8 when he promised, "If I have cheated anybody out of anything, I will pay back four times the amount.")

In the Gospels, tax collectors are repeatedly associated with or equated to sinners. Matthew 11:19 speaks of Jesus as "a friend of tax collectors and sinners" (NIV). In Luke 5:30 the Pharisees ask the disciples of Jesus, "Why do you eat and drink with tax collectors and sinners?" (NIV). Luke 15:1 clearly places Jesus in the midst of such people: "Now the tax collectors and sinners were all gathering around to hear Jesus" (NIV). Tax collectors were despised and viewed with contempt by almost everyone in the first-century Jewish world.

Actually, another tax collector was already among Jesus' closest followers. Matthew traveled alongside another outsider, a zealot by the name of Simon. Based on the twelve men named in Luke 6:12-16, Jesus seemed to be pushing for diversity and conflict resolution from the start. He drafted into his group of disciples two men who occupied polar opposite positions within their community—one who was perceived to be a collaborator with Rome against his own people and the other a zealot who was committed to the destruction of Roman rule in his homeland, probably beginning with collaborators such as the tax collectors.

Jesus invited himself to dinner in the home of Zacchaeus, who was the chief tax collector in the region of Jericho (Luke 19:1-10). Zacchaeus was undoubtedly a member of the Jewish community in terms of ethnicity, but he was outside that community because of his vocation. Luke 19:7 points to that status: "All the people saw this and began to mutter, 'He has gone to be the guest of a sinner'" (NIV).

But because Jesus refused to remain safely within the walls of acceptable social interaction, something wonderful happened. When Jesus was willing to enter into his world, Zacchaeus was restored to the family of faith (as "a son of Abraham"). He repented of his sins and resolved to make restitution to those he had wronged. Most importantly, he became the case study concerning which Jesus spoke the words that should light a fire for a third-circle of care ministry in every local church in the world: "For the Son of Man came to seek and to save the lost" (Luke 19:10, NIV).

How can the church join with Jesus in seeking and saving that which is lost unless and until the church moves beyond the comfort zone of its own building and membership and intentionally moves outward into the world that waits beyond its doors? Call it having an external focus or being a village church, but practicing this third-circle care is not a task we should undertake out of some sense of burden or unwanted duty. It should be seized upon because such interventions can have redemptive and transformative outcomes for those whose lives are touched by the care and concern of the church.

How do we want the Lord to find us? Will the Lord find us working as an externally focused village church that is seeking to make a positive difference in the world? Or will the Lord find us introverted and locked away behind the walls of our sanctuary waiting to serve any and all members in good standing of the congregation who walk through our doors into the church? If the latter option is the one we choose, then we may realize the same fate as the rich man who died and awoke in hell all because he failed to show any concern or compassion for the people and problems just outside his gate (Luke 16:19-31).

Notes

1. Eddie Glaude Jr., "The Black Church Is Dead" (February 24, 2010), www.huffingtonpost.com/eddie-glaude-jr-phd/the-black-church-is-dead_b_473815.html (accessed July 5, 2011), 1.

2. Glaude, 1

3. Glaude, 1

4. Glaude, 1

5. Rick Rusaw and Eric Swanson, *The Externally Focused Church* (Loveland, CO: Group, 2004), 24.

6. Rusaw and Swanson, 24.

7. Rusaw and Swanson, 25.

8. Paul Nixon, *Fling Open the Doors: Giving the Church Away to the Community* (Nashville: Abingdon, 2002), 22.

9. Nixon, 22.

10. Nixon, 22.

11. Sam Dolnick, "Brooklyn Immigrant Congregations Clash," *New York Times* Reprints, December 28, 2010, 1

12. Dolnick, 1.

CHAPTER 12

Two Churches in One Building

*Finally, all of you, be like-minded, be sympathetic, love
one another, be compassionate and humble.*
—1 Peter 3:8 (NIV)

How can a local church begin the process of establishing a third
circle of care? With so many needs in our communities and so
many broken people outside our doors, how can a congregation
identify the areas of pastoral care ministry that God is calling them
to address? What philosophy or principle of ministry can be used
to envision and undergird such an effort?

More than twenty years ago, our church in the heart of the city
of Cleveland, Ohio, adopted a concept we call "two churches in
one building." I first wrote about that concept in my book
Preaching to the Black Middle Class:

> Most inner city churches serve two rarely interconnecting
> groups. One comprises congregants who gather once or
> twice a week for a couple of hours and then leave with lit-
> tle or no contact with the people who actually live in those
> communities. The other consists of persons in the immedi-
> ate vicinity of the church building who are virtual clients.
> They gather on a daily basis for a hot meal, a meeting of a
> twelve-step program that aids in the battle against drugs

and alcohol, or help in navigating the complexities of some government bureaucracies.[1]

The discussion of inner-city churches reaching out to the people in their surrounding communities continued with this observation:

> The challenge for inner-city churches is to offer meaning-ful and supportive ministries, both pastoral and program-matic, to the two groups of people—the middle class members who commute to the church and the increasing-ly impoverished people who live in the neighborhood in which the church building is located....These churches will have to find ways to do ministry that is relevant and empowering for both groups.[2]

This concept of two churches in one building was also important as our congregation sought to expand our outreach ministries into the community that surrounds our building. It took some time for this idea to catch on, but eventually our worshipping church members came to see that the reason they were paying their tithes and offerings was to equip and empower the church to better serve the people and problems in the surrounding community. One of the ways by which that outreach has been occurring for the last twen-ty years has been by inviting nonmembers of the congregation to see the church facilities as resources that are open and available to the surrounding neighborhood and the wider community for a multitude of purposes and programs.

Needless to say, persons from the community are always invited to and welcome at all of our worship services and other congrega-tional events. Many members of the surrounding community have either joined the church or started attending on a regular basis. However, our mission through outreach is not primarily evangel-ism and church growth. Our mission is pastoral care—the ministry of extending the love and concern of Jesus Christ beyond the membership of our congregation and beyond the walls of our church building.

Your Ministry Should Reflect Your Neighborhood

Churches should shape their third-circle of care ministries with a clear sense of who lives and what operates just outside their doors. What is needed in one neighborhood may not be appropriate or necessary in another. The fact that one church has had great success with some form of ministry within their radius of influence does not mean the same ministry would work in any other church located in any other part of town. The third circle of care should be designed with a clear awareness of the people and problems that reside just outside the door of your local church.

For instance, ministry within the poverty-ridden inner-city of Cleveland, Ohio, would likely not be the same as the forms of ministry that might be developed in the more affluent suburban communities that are located only five to ten miles beyond the city limits. Indeed, there is every likelihood that ministries carried out by certain churches in the inner-city may not be necessary even for churches located elsewhere within the city limits. Churches should appropriate a line from Booker T. Washington's famous and controversial speech of 1895, "Cast down your buckets where you are."[3]

The phrase "just outside your doors" should not be restricted only to those who happen to live across the street or around the corner from your church. As I said in chapter 11, Paul Nixon says that the phrase "just outside your doors" points to "the geographic area for which the church takes responsibility," however wide that area might be.[4] Many suburban congregations may not have the same diversity and intensity of needs (what may be called a "misery index") within walking distance of their local church, so they may choose to extend their love and concern to people living in nearby towns and cities where the misery index is far more intense.

A partnership between a suburban church and an urban congregation may be highly effective—not only in enriching discipleship for all church members but in meeting the needs of the neighbors whom all would agree are considered "least of these."

Problems Vary from One Neighborhood to Another

That being said, it must be remembered that the catalog of human suffering is not the exclusive burden of those people and congregations located within our nation's inner-cities. Poverty is an issue in rural communities; illiteracy runs rampant in city and country alike. Substance abuse, domestic violence, dysfunctional family relationships, and mental health issues are increasingly—and even equally—common in the middle-class suburbs. Divorce, home foreclosures, unexpected unemployment, and adolescent peer pressure are daily realities across the socioeconomic spectrum in North America. The middle and upper classes may have resources to cover the cost of their medical care, but insurance cannot keep their aging parents from developing Alzheimer's disease, exempt their spouses from a diagnosis of colon cancer, or protect their babies from sudden infant death syndrome. Wealth is no safeguard against an accidental shooting, a house fire, the explosion of a natural gas pipeline, or the collapse of a stock portfolio following fraudulent actions by the Bernard Madoffs of the world. Human suffering can be found in even the best neighborhoods.

Suburban and more outlying areas that were created to provide some distance from the pressures of urban life now find themselves struggling to cope with the encroachments of persons living in poverty, renters instead of home owners, and the aggravations of absentee landlords. The crime rate is increasing in suburban areas, especially rape and robbery, which are often perpetrated by persons living within those communities. These are just some of the areas in which local churches in affluent communities might be able to offer a third circle of care to persons whose lives seemed secure one minute but were turned upside down in the twinkling of an eye.

So if your church is located in one of those "better" communities, don't automatically look to your nearest urban centers for a place in which to do ministry. Drive around your own neighborhood first. Pay attention to the local news and attend your town's council and school board meetings. Talk with local business owners, and sit down with the principals of your area elementary and high schools. You are likely to learn all too quickly that your suburban paradise has fractures in its social, economic, political, and educational systems. You will probably discover all too many broken people living in gated homes and high-priced condos, offering your congregation a multitude of areas in which to make yourselves useful in the service of God. The "slings and arrows of outrageous fortune" come flying at the doors of affluent homes as well. Thus, there is an urgent need for a third circle of care to be extended in every community in our nation.

Sometimes Our Circle of Care Is Too Narrow

A special responsibility falls to pastors and churches serving in communities of power and privilege or serving city churches where persons of power and influence regularly attend. Some people living in those communities and worshipping in those churches are insulated from the pain and oppression experienced every day by persons who may live only a few miles away from them. Decades and even centuries of prejudice involving race, gender, ethnicity, sexual preference, and other forms of diversity continue to rage within our nation, and many persons of power and privilege remain unconcerned about the suffering that occurs just outside the doors of their homes.

One of the worst sins of our society—and it is as true in affluent areas as it is anywhere else—is the sin of silence when some injustice occurs within society. In his *Letter from the Birmingham Jail* written in 1963, Martin Luther King Jr. was actually chiding eight white clergymen in Birmingham, Alabama, for being part of a conspiracy of silence over the awful practices of segregation. He also chided them for their silence in the face of the brutal violence that was being employed by public safety forces to maintain that racist status quo. Those eight clergyman and the congregations they represented were not affected or impacted by the harsh segregation laws that governed Birmingham in 1963, and they did not seem concerned about the way in which those regulations insulted or dehumanized the black citizens of Birmingham.

Here is a small sampling of the segregation codes that Martin Luther King Jr. came to Birmingham to challenge, resulting in his being chastised by those eight faith leaders.

■ It shall be unlawful to conduct a restaurant or other place for the service of food in the city, at which white and colored people are served in the same room, unless such white and colored people are effectually separated by a solid partition extending from the floor upward to a distance of seven feet or higher, and unless a separate entrance from the street is provided for each compartment.[5]

■ It shall be unlawful for a negro and a white person to play together or in company with each other in any game of cards or dice, dominoes, checkers, baseball, softball, football, basketball, or similar games.[6]

■ It shall be unlawful for any person, contrary to the provisions of this section providing for equal and separate accommodations for the white and colored races on streetcars, to ride or attempt to ride in a car or a division of a car designated for the race to which such person does not belong.[7] Segregation was extended to include: "Any room, hall theatre, picture house, auditorium, yard, court, ballpark, public park, or other outdoor or indoor place to which both white persons and negroes are admitted."[8] (Note that so-called negroes were not considered persons.)

That is what led Dr. King to say, "We will have to repent in this generation not merely for the hateful words and actions of the bad people but for the appalling silence of the good people. Human progress never rolls in on the wheels of inevitability; it comes through the tireless efforts of men willing to be co-workers with God, and without this hard work, time itself becomes an ally of the forces of social stagnation."[9]

What bothered King was that those eight religious leaders (Protestant, Catholic, and Jewish) were certainly aware of those laws and regulations, but they seemed to have no objections to how the black population was being treated. They sat by and observed these cruel regulations being enforced, sometimes through the use of fire hoses and police dogs turned against those who were working for a more just society. Those white clergypersons that were no doubt faithful in the service they rendered in the first two circles of pastoral care seemed ignorant of or indifferent to what they observed every day in restaurants, theaters, public parks, buses, and railroad cars—remaining silent while others suffered. King described such persons as "white moderates that are more devoted to 'order' than to justice; who prefer a negative peace which is the absence of tension to a positive peace which is the presence of justice."[10]

The white clergy and the white faith communities are not so different from many white clergy and white faith communities all across this country in the twenty-first century. Here in Ohio, a newly elected governor appointed an all-white twenty-three-member cabinet that heads all the major departments of state government.[11] While many black clergy and black Christians were in an uproar about this blatant disregard for diversity or inclusion, most white clergy and most white people of any faith tradition have yet to say a word or offer a helping hand in trying to reverse this return to the appearance of 1950s American government.

The sin of silence in the face of injustice continues to this day. The truth is, too many churches and too many pastors of all racial and ethnic backgrounds have become too comfortable and too conditioned to a wide range of acts and attitudes of cruelty, injustice, and prejudice that occur in our nation every day. Too many in the church remain silent in the face of a multitude of issues well beyond race. We are silent about senseless homophobia. We are silent about the sexual exploitation of women and children. We are silent about the impact of failing school systems on children who have no other option than public schools. We are silent about the high costs of war both in terms of money and human capital. We are silent about the millions of people who are living without medical insurance. We are silent about the staggering rate of incarceration in our nation's jails and prisons. We are silent about the abuse of migrant workers and the exploitation of undocumented immigrants. We are silent about the way state and federal budgets are being balanced on the backs of poor and working-class people. We are just too silent! That is some of what we must overcome in our churches if we are to be able to provide that third circle of care that so many of "our neighbors" need.

Evangelism Must Be Partnered with Empathy

The ministries that we perform should be done in the right spirit and for the right reason. The sense of responsibility that we should feel for a given geographical area should be based as much on our empathy concerning the physical and existential condition of those who live there as it is on our desire to engage in the work of evangelism. We should be as quick to exhibit a spirit of service as we are to engage in the work of solicitation that might result in church growth. We should be as clearly focused on exhibiting the traits of discipleship as we are on any effort to expand our church membership.

Why would people in the neighborhoods around our churches want to join our membership if our entire ministry has been and remains introverted and focused only on those who already "belong" to our congregation? In truth, it is unlikely that the people living in the communities surrounding our churches would ever find their way into the local church of which they are not presently members if there has been no attempt by those who are members of that church to open their doors, extend their hands, and reach out in a loving and caring way. People are not likely to storm the walls of a fortress church that has spent decades paying no attention to the people and problems that reside just outside its doors.

Learn a Lesson from Paul

Remember Paul Nixon's challenge to assume some responsibility for what happens or does not happen within our designated geographical area? Our church members should not have to be the victims of injustice themselves before we get involved. As Jesus did repeatedly, we need to expand our understanding of who is our neighbor and come to their aid whether we share in their pain or not. That is precisely the impulse of empathy the apostle Paul called for when he said, "Rejoice with those who rejoice; mourn with those who mourn" (Roman 12:15, NIV).

We should be happy for those who are happy because they have experienced some great blessing, even if nothing like that has occurred in our lives. Similarly, we should weep with those who are weeping or show concern and empathy for those who are passing through a time of hardship and sorrow. This is the heart of the third circle of care; it reaches beyond the walls of our local church to those people and problems that are found within the geographical area for which we take some responsibility. Our local church ministries should be shaped, funded, and executed with all of this in mind.

Our Responses Should Be Relevant and Relational

Make every effort to ensure that your love and care are tailored to address the real problems of the community. Don't limit your responses to those that are easiest to achieve but have the least likelihood of having any lasting impact on the community. A third circle of care is not defined by the benevolent impulses of well-meaning Christians who believe that a soup kitchen, food bank, and "lightly worn" clothing exchange are the full extent of what it means to love one's neighbor. In addition to those standard programs, a great many other forms of ministry might be needed in the neighborhood for which your church has assumed some responsibility.

Depending on the needs of your community, third-circle care ministries may include marriage enrichment or parenting seminars, before- and after-school programs with tutoring or mentoring, Alcoholics or Narcotics Anonymous support groups, financial planning and debt consolidation workshops, tangible assistance with emergency needs such as food or prescription medications, and support for persons infected with or affected by HIV/AIDS. This last example might include access to testing services, counseling for those who test positive, current information about treatment plans, and practical support for those for whom HIV/AIDS has become a chronic disease that requires a daily regimen of medication. At Antioch Baptist Church, we started an HIV/AIDS ministry called AGAPE. The Koine Greek word for God's unconditional love became for us an acronym for awareness, growth, action, programs, and education. Churches would do well to employ both approaches to the word *agape*.

Other third-circle ministries may involve forms of advocacy for persons dealing with local, state, and federal government bureaucracies. Some churches partner with local law enforcement agencies in gun buy-backs and a program called Fugitive Safe Surrender, in which persons with an outstanding felony warrant can turn themselves in as part of a prearranged program hosted by a local church. That has greatly reduced the number of violent encounters between law enforcement groups and fugitives seeking to avoid apprehension. Felons are living and hiding in all parts of our society, and such a church-based program would serve a useful purpose whether held in the inner-city or in a suburban church sanctuary.

There is an urgent need for adult literacy programs, for health fairs that screen for breast and prostate cancer, and for support groups for ex-offenders upon their release and for their families while they are still incarcerated. If your congregation has a passion for ministry with prisoners, invest the extra time and effort required to hold a worship service inside the jails and prisons of your county or state. Establish relationships with individual inmates and keep in touch with the institutional chaplain if one exists. And when those inmates become eligible for parole, your church members may have the privilege of testifying at their hearings and facilitating their transition back into home, church, and community life. Such a ministry is a blessing as much for the church members and community residents as it is for the returning citizens, their families, and the personnel who work in the prisons and jails.

The View from 89th and Cedar

When thinking about what a third circle of pastoral care might involve, churches would do well to take a careful assessment of the real world condition of the people and problems in their immediate and surrounding neighborhoods. In some circles, this would be called an environmental scan. If the rich man in Luke 16:19-31 had taken the time to take a careful look at what was happening just outside his door, he would have seen Lazarus—hungry, covered in sores, and impoverished. The first and most important step toward a third circle of care is an honest assessment of how and where such care needs to be directed.

For instance, within a one-mile radius of 89th and Cedar, the location of the church where I serve as senior pastor, you can find heightened amounts of every misery index that can be imagined. Cleveland has been listed on several occasions as the poorest big city in the United States. If that fact is true, then Antioch Baptist Church is located in one of the poorest neighborhoods in the poorest city in America. Of the adult residents in Ward Six (the Fairfax community), 45 percent live at or below the poverty level. That number swells to over 60 percent of school-age children. That is the neighborhood for which we are challenged to assume some responsibility.

Poverty increases rates of domestic violence, drug and alcohol abuse, criminality, and incarceration. (In fact, a new county juvenile jail and court are currently being constructed within that same one mile radius.) Because poverty often results in home foreclosures, we are seeing an increase in homelessness. The high school dropout rate is increasing, as is gang activity.

With the industrial heydays of the twenty-first century behind us, Cleveland and other cities, such as Detroit, Chicago, and Pittsburgh, are having to reinvent themselves with new industries and businesses, often in banking or some other high-tech area that would have no position available for a person who had not even finished high school. That makes providing literacy programs and job interview training, helping to expunge criminal records, writing letters of reference, and working with local employers to provide entry-level positions important services of our third circle of care.

Consider the Demographics Inside Your Church Too— Thus far I have focused on the demographics *outside* and surrounding our church at 89th and Cedar. The next step in planning a third circle of pastoral care is to give careful attention to the demographics *within* the church walls. While our church building is located in the inner-city of Cleveland, the vast majority of church members live outside that immediate neighborhood. In fact, more than 50 percent of the membership resides outside the city of Cleveland.

While they attend a church in Cleveland and come into the city for an occasional professional sports event or a musical concert, most of them have no other involvement with or attachment to the city, its people, or its problems. They are good people seeking to live out the American dream for themselves and their children. That being said, they too can begin to overlook or choose to ignore the suffering that they see as they are driving to and from church each week. Sound familiar?

That is why caring pastors must take steps to develop a philosophy of ministry that calls for the direct involvement of members in the ministries that impact the people and problems in our surrounding communities. With such a philosophy, church members become more than worshippers and tithers; they become assets and resources that can be identified and employed in various areas of the work of the church.

For instance, challenge lawyers within the church to make their services available on some rotating pro bono basis for persons in the neighborhood around the church. These services might include providing legal advice about wills, powers of attorney, and health care proxies; interpreting and responding to court orders loaded with specialized legal terms; and assisting with specific issues, ranging from expunging juvenile records to pursuing child or spousal support and filing protective orders against abusers. Encourage retired and active teachers to offer tutoring services in their field of expertise. Invite physicians and dentists to offer health screenings and provide educational programs that address a variety of health concerns. Ask funeral directors to provide seminars on planning for the high costs of death and dying. Urge bankers and financial advisers to host workshops on financial literacy, predatory lending, and credit repair. Dispatch executives from corporate America to high school career days to talk about the steps that lead to success in business.

Where Your Treasure Is, There Your Heart Is Also—For most congregations, central to your third circle of care will be the commitment to design an annual budget with an outward focus in mind. In addition to the volunteer efforts of members of our congregation, our aspirations to reach out to our community with love and concern need to be supported by the financial resources of our congregation as well.

At Antioch Baptist Church, we operate on the principle of dual tithing. First, we invite members of the congregation to tithe to the church 10 percent of their annual income. Second, we commit to tithe to the community—giving 10 percent of the church's annual income through direct financial support to local groups and agencies that provide a wide variety of services, including the NAACP, adult literacy programs, drug rehabilitation centers, clothing exchanges, hunger centers and food delivery programs, youth mentoring activities, ecumenical and interfaith efforts, and ministry activities on local college campuses, just to name a few. Even through tough economic times, both in the nation and within our church, we do not make cuts in this part of our budget. We will make cuts that impact our members before we make cuts in areas that significantly impact our ministry.

As described in chapter 1, our church is organized around the concept of TOWER, an acronym for teaching, outreach, worship, evangelism, and relationships. Most of our second-circle ministries occur under the rubric of relationships—with members caring for one another. Most of our third-circle ministries occur under the heading of outreach—with the congregation caring for the wider community. In your church, the third-circle of care budget might address the following areas of outreach and care:

■ Denominational support
■ Community outreach (including civil rights groups, nursing homes, neighborhood centers, support groups, prison and reentry ministries, etc.)
■ Education outreach (including campus ministry, adult literacy programs, scholarship programs, tutoring, English as a second language classes, etc.)
■ Faith-based associations (including theological education)
■ Hunger outreach (including food pantry, holiday baskets, hot meal programs, etc.)

Some congregations pursue third-circle care through faith-based organizations distinct from the church operating or mission budget. Some churches will partner with existing outside organizations; other congregations will do as we have done at Antioch and create their own 501(c)3 tax-exempt entity that allows the church to receive grants from foundations, government agencies, and corporations. The church budget often subsidizes such an entity, whether the entity is a church-related school, a counseling center, a medical clinic, or a tutoring center.

The Antioch Development Corporation (ADC) is our 501(c)3, and through its resources we support (among other programs) our HIV/AIDS ministry, AGAPE. We make every effort to conduct our AIDS ministry in the spirit of *agape* love, not in the spirit of judgment or condemnation. Our focus is AIDS prevention, and in 2010 AGAPE provided counseling and testing to 2,589 at-risk adults. AGAPE also sponsors a teen-focused program called Stopping AIDS Is My Mission (SAMM). That program provided HIV prevention education to 1,818 eleventh and twelfth grade students of the Cleveland Metropolitan School District.[12] Sadly, few churches are involved in this area of ministry, but the need continues to increase.

Your Facility Is a Partner in Your Ministry— The third circle of pastoral care is not limited to the way in which the congregation reaches out to the community outside its church walls. A great deal of third-circle care can occur when persons from the community are invited to take advantage of programs and services provided inside the church building itself. The love of Jesus Christ at work in the hearts of Christians may move in an outward direction, but the programs offered as an extension of that love may actually work best when the church building becomes the context and setting in which much of this ministry takes place.

For example, some churches have strict policies when it comes to who is allowed to have their funeral service in the church. (Only active members in good standing are extended that opportunity.) Other congregations recognize that their facility can provide a ministry for nonmembers who would like to use the sanctuary for a funeral service—especially if the deceased was a member of a smaller church that doesn't have the seating capacity for the anticipated crowd of mourners. Such hospitality during a time of bereavement is a third-circle act of care.

Similarly, churches with a baptismal pool may be called on to make that pool available to another church that does not have a pool but does have candidates who desire baptism by immersion. Churches with a commercial kitchen and spacious social hall may be asked to open those facilities to families or groups in the community for family reunions, organizational dinner meetings, or for a hot meal program that feeds the hungry within a certain radius of the building.

Tutoring programs, financial literacy training, voter education and registration projects, candidate forums, community-wide holiday events, police-civilian forums following some violent encounter, and presentations by the local school district about issues of funding and/or programs are just a sampling of the events that can be hosted inside a church with a third-circle of care mentality. These churches can also sponsor health fairs and screenings inside their buildings. Unused classrooms in the education wing can become computer labs for neighborhood children or adult learners. Grief support groups for the mothers of murdered children would welcome access to a church for their meetings. The same is true for the families of prisoners, who often meet to support and encourage one another, as well as for returning citizens looking for a community of support upon their release from prison and reentry into society.

While Problems Increase, Government Support Is Declining
At a time when more and more people are in need of assistance with food, housing, employment, tuition, affordable medical coverage, transportation costs, child-care expenses, and so much more, the resources of local and state governments are shrinking. In Ohio the state faces an $8 billion budget deficit. That number is even larger in some other states across the country. In an attempt to close those budget gaps, governors and state legislatures are looking for cost savings wherever they can be found or made.

This reality raises two challenges for externally focused, or village, churches that are engaged in a third circle of pastoral care. First, pastors and church leaders must serve as the conscience of the community when cost-cutting plans are being developed. That may mean sitting in on meetings when those discussions are being held or writing the appropriate legislative bodies to express concerns in this area. Unless we keep a close watch on that budget-cutting process, much of the cost savings will come at the expense of programs that serve the needs of our poorest and most vulnerable citizens. Keeping watch on budgets is a legitimate and necessary expression of third-circle care and concern.

The second challenge that dwindling government support raises for churches is the need to step up and fill in the gaps by providing social services. As governments are forced to do less, churches will be among the faith-based organizations called on to do more with the resources available to them. This will require a redefinition of the term *faith-based*. In most places, *faith-based* simply means religious organizations that run programs funded by government, charitable, or foundation dollars. In that context, *faith-based* references only the nature of the organizations in which the services are provided. We are quickly coming to a time when *faith-based* must take on an entirely new meaning, especially where the use of the word *faith* is concerned.

In a time of dwindling support from other sources, churches are going to have to start running our programs on faith, believing that if we step out on faith to serve God's people, God will honor that faith and raise up persons who will assist in the funding and operation of those programs and ministries. This may require that our ministries operate with less overhead in terms of paid staff. The role of volunteers may need to be expanded. Increased donations of food, financial support, and professional expertise may be required from the members of the local church. Several congregations may need to partner with one another to address issues that no one congregation can resolve alone. Most of all, a new paradigm on how to approach the work of ministry will certainly be necessary as we move further into the twenty-first century.

Notes

1. Marvin A. McMickle, *Preaching to the Black Middle Class* (Valley Forge, PA: Judson Press, 2000), 2.

2. McMickle, 2.

3. Booker T. Washington, "The Friendship of the Two Races," in *Historic Speeches of African Americans* (New York: Watts, 1993), 81–86.

4. Paul Nixon, *Fling Open the Doors: Giving the Church Away to the Community* (Nashville: Abingdon, 2002), 18.

5. Birmingham's Racial Segregation Ordinances, distributed by the Birmingham Civil Rights Institute, 520 Sixteenth St. N, Birmingham, AL, p. 1, ordinance #597.

6. Birmingham, 1, ordinance #798-F.

7. Birmingham, 3, ordinance #1002.

8. Birmingham, 2, ordinance #359.

9. Martin Luther King Jr., *Why We Can't Wait* (New York: Signet, 1964), 86.

10. King, 84.

11. Reginald Fields, "Democrats Rip Kasich's All-White Cabinet," *The Plain Dealer*, January 28, 2011, 1.

12. Antioch Baptist Church Annual Report, Outreach Ministry, Minister Kelvin Berry, Director (January 31, 2011), 55.

Third-Circle Questions for Consideration

1. What ministries and programs does your local church sponsor that focus on a third circle of care, beyond your walls and beyond your membership?

2. Who are the people just outside your church doors and what issues and problems do they face that would benefit from third-circle ministries?

3. What biblical arguments can you make for why churches should be involved in a third-circle ministry?

4. How do you understand the phrase *externally focused church*? On a scale of 1 to 10, how externally focused is your congregation?

5. How do you see the issue of interfaith or multifaith activity within your community?

6. To what extent does your pastor meet resistance when he or she invites the congregation to care for the surrounding community?

7. What group constitutes "the stranger" or the Samaritan in your community? How does your congregation reach out to that group, if at all?

8. Do you agree with Eddie Glaude that the church in the United States is dead in terms of its influence on the broader society? Why or why not?

9. According to Paul Nixon, what does it mean to be a village church? To what extent does your congregation function as a village church?

10. What does it mean to have two churches in one building? Does that concept reflect the ministries of your local church? Why or why not?

CONCLUSION

Pastoral and Congregational Imagination

Throughout this book, I have made an appeal for pastors and congregations to rethink how we consider and conduct the ministries of the local church. Caring pastors work to give shape to a caring congregation that shows love and concern not only for the members of their own local church, but also for the people and problems that reside beyond the doors of their church building. One other ministry principle that might aid pastors and churches in adopting the idea of the three concentric circles of pastoral care is what Diana Butler Bass calls "imagining a new old church."[1]

This is a concept that allows an old and established church with a long tradition of doing things in a certain way to begin to imagine that things can and should be done differently. The first step, says Bass, is "pastoral imagination." This is a term she borrows from an article by Craig Dykstra.[2] Dykstra insists that "good pastors must have clear awareness and analytical understanding of the world that the church exists to serve, both locally and in relationship to the larger environment in which it operates."[3] He continues by saying that pastoral imagination involves a pastor "who has a way of seeing into and interpreting the world that reaches from the inner places of the human heart, through the congregation, out to the world, and back again."[4]

Seminary faculties, including the one on which I serve at Ashland Theological Seminary in Ohio, as well as Colgate Rochester Crozer Divinity School where I was elected to serve as president in 2011, would also do well to remember the importance of pastoral imagination. In addition to courses in Bible, history, theology, and ministry practices, we should be certain that we are also equipping our students with pastoral imagination that will allow them to put their professional training to work with maximum benefit in and for the contexts in which they will be serving. Failure to have this pastoral imagination, says Bass, is to have clergy that have expertise in preaching and stewardship and other church-based programs "but that lack a powerful sense of vocation in a world that needs grace and mercy."[5]

In addition to pastoral imagination, which is the ministry vision the pastor brings before a congregation, Bass also calls for "congregational imagination, which is the ability of a local church to see beyond the walls of their church buildings in order to understand their sacred location in both the longer story of American religious history and the contemporary quest for spiritual meaning."[6] When taken together, pastoral imagination and congregational imagination "are two different angles of vocational calling and vision, one from the pulpit and the other from the pew, of a common spiritual gift of seeing God at work and embodying faith, hope, and love in the world."[7]

This is exactly what the three concentric circles of pastoral care entail. They begin with pastoral imagination as pastors work not only to perform those tasks assigned to them by professional training and ordination, but as they understand that part of their task is to equip the church to do the work of the ministry (Ephesians 4:11-13). If clergy cannot imagine a church in which the members are working together with the pastor both inside and outside the walls of their local church, then it is not likely that the three concentric circles of pastoral care will ever take shape within that church.

On the other hand, failure at ministry as it is being discussed here is equally probable if the congregation cannot imagine a form of ministry in which they are all actively involved with the pastor in ways that occur both inside and outside the walls of their local church. Christianity is not a spectator sport in which the congregation sits in the pews while the pastor and other clergy invoke the lyrics of an old rock-and-roll song by the Contours that says, "Watch me work."

The local church must have congregational imagination that will allow it to be like the villagers in Bethany who were already at the home of Mary and Martha following the death of Lazarus, even before Jesus arrived to raise him from the dead. Congregational imagination means that the local church is like the four unnamed men who worked to bring a paralytic into the presence of Jesus in Capernaum, and whose great faith as exhibited by how they tore open the roof and lowered the man down into the room resulted in that paralytic being able to stand and walk. Congregational imagination will allow the church to avoid the fate of the rich man who ended up in hell because he did not show love and concern for the poor, sick beggar who sat just outside his gate.

God forbid that any pastor or the members of any congregation should go to church all their lives and still end up in hell. Such a thing can happen unless there is both pastoral and congregational imagination shaping a ministry that involves members caring for one another inside their church and that also challenges those members to show love and concern for the people and problems in the geographical area for which their local church is prepared to assume some responsibility.

Notes

1. Diana Butler Bass, *The Practicing Congregation: Imagining a New Old Church* (Herndon, VA: Alban Institute, 2004), 5–6.

2. Craig Dykstra, "Pastoral Imagination," *Initiatives in Religion* 9, no. 1 (Spring 2001): 2.

3. Dykstra, 5.

4. Dykstra, 5.

5. Bass, 6.

6. Bass, 5–6.

7. Bass, 6.